THE SPORTING COLLECTOR

Previous books by the author include:

Newmarket
Golf with Your Hands
Swing to Better Golf
Grand Prix World Championship
Lawn Tennis
Los Campeones de Tenis en Accion
Rugby Football
Pelham Golf Year
The Cambridge Year
Journey Through Cornwall
The Old Inns of London
Life in Cambridge
Germany After the War
The Sunday Book
The University City of Cambridge
The Beauty of Woman
The London Season
Master Golfers in Action
Green Fairways
Fresh Fairways
The B.R.M. Story
People, Places and Pleasures
The Golfers' Bedside Book
Collecting Staffordshire Pottery
Motor Racing (1–12)

THE SPORTING COLLECTOR

by

Louis T. Stanley

PELHAM BOOKS

LONDON

First published in Great Britain by
Pelham Books Ltd
44 Bedford Square
London WC1B 3DP
1984

British Library Cataloguing in Publication Data

Stanley, Louis
    The sporting collector.
    1. Sports—Collectibles
    I.   Title
    796'.076   GV568.5

ISBN 0-7207-1545-8

Filmset, printed and bound in Great Britain by
Butler & Tanner Limited, Frome and London

CONTENTS

CHAPTER I

THE SPORTING TRADITION

'How for everything there is a time and a season and then how does the glory of a thing pass from it even like the flower of the grass.' These words were written by George Borrow of the glories of the prize-ring. They apply with equal force to the innumerable sports and pastimes of the British people. Sporting pursuits are subject to the wiles of fashion. A wave of popularity may recede until it becomes the veriest trickle of a placid backwater. The prize-ring was such an instance. It faded out completely. The brutal streak disappeared, making way for the more restrained version of boxing, but interest in the old fighters remains. One of the most deeply rooted things in the English character is the love of sailors and prize-fighters. 'Almost everybody in our land, except humanitarians and a few persons whose youth had been depressed by exceptional aesthetic surroundings, can understand and sympathise with an admiral or a prize-fighter. I do not wish to bracket Benbow and Tom Crib; but, depend upon it, they are practically bracketed for admiration in the minds of many frequenters of alehouses. If you told them about Germanicus and the eagles, or Regulus going back to Carthage, they would very likely fall asleep, but tell them about Harry Pearce and Jim Belcher, or about Nelson and the Nile, and they put down their pipes to listen.' Thus spoke Stevenson.

The sporting canvas is so vast and varied that it baffles the enquiring eye of a single observer or collector. Even those whose minds form an epitome of selective sports find difficulty in discerning the complete picture. England has many interpreters, and I use the term 'England' in its fullest sense. Those who visit these islands take away a composite memory of the English scene. The country is split up into its component parts of villages, towns, fields, woods, hills and rivers with the ever-near sound of the sea as background music. The weakness of such an

impression is obvious to an Englishman. England to her people means different things.

To appreciate the part that sport plays in our national life it is helpful to attempt what is virtually the impossible: namely, to convey to a stranger who does not know us what the scenes that he sees from the carriage window as a train bisects the counties means to those who have known them from childhood. The chalk-stream, the weir, and the falls of a river are more than scenery to an angler. Fields of clover and roots, the mists of a bog or the loneliness of the moor are the natural habitat of the shooting-man. The stranger will be forgiven if he thinks of Canterbury, Worcester, Taunton and Tonbridge as centres with varying degrees of tourist appeal. That is true, but these names mean far more to an Englishman.

The cricketer looks at the calendar. He knows that as spring is breaking into bud so new bats and flannels will be making an appearance. The season begins in an intermittent way, gradually blooming into the fullness of maturity in summer, to fade when the trees are brown. Those days seem far away. In the meantime, the rich sequence of names like Canterbury, Worcester, Taunton and Tonbridge holds promise of hours to come when cricket grounds will resound to the impact of leather on willow. I admit it doesn't sound much to a non-cricketer. For that reason alone, how can a stranger in our midst hope to find himself in sympathy with pursuits so native to our soil? It has become a truism to say that cricket is part of the Englishman's heritage, yet in essence the sentiment is true. Cricket as such is a game that needs England and an English summer to come to fruition. It is within the power of the sporting collector to summon such moments from the past.

I have touched but the fringe of the sporting season. In a way, the background remains the same, yet for each there is outlined a separate English vignette. In any attempt to describe sporting England the memory can only deal with those things that have held one in thought. The result has to be an individualistic reflection and the same goes for associated memorabilia.

Had I the task of escorting a stranger through the sporting calendar, I should begin with the Boat Race. From several points of view, it is an

(*opposite*): One day each year the Thames becomes the joint property of Oxford and Cambridge for the Boat Race.

extraordinary spectacle. Here is evidence, if such be needed, of the Englishman's love of sport. Over four miles of riverbank form a grandstand for thousands of spectators. Few have any real allegiance to either Oxford or Cambridge, yet partisan feeling is rife. To this total must be added the vast number who follow the race by means of radio, television, and newspaper columns. The art of rowing is a highly specialised sport. Only the smallest fraction of this interested public knows anything about the Fairbairn style, sliding-seats, or have even been in a boat. Love of tradition is part of the answer. This race has been rowed since 1829. In the midst of London, on the best-loved of our rivers, the two oldest universities combine to provide a water carnival of sport. As a spectacle, the eight-oared crews demonstrate perfect co-ordination of grace and vigour under complete control. The Commemorative Plate and Mug issued to mark the 150th anniversary of the race give a detailed record from its inaugural struggle as well as period-detail of spectators at that first meeting.

The next event would be the Grand National, if only to show that English sporting crowds can be cosmopolitan to the core. This is more marked at Aintree than on Epsom Downs. It is a blending of cross-country enthusiasts with flat-racing specialists as befits a meeting recognised by both the Jockey Club and the National Hunt. No one can question the courage or staying-power of man or beast who attempts to conquer this pear-shaped course with thirty formidable jumps. Anyone who completes the course has proved his quality to the world.

Then in contrast we go to the other extreme, the premier out-of-doors social function of the season – Royal Ascot. There are not many places left in England that can be labelled aristocratic. There is no reason to be ashamed about such a tag. In spite of certain elements, England is still a monarchical country with an aristocracy. Not so many years ago this could be seen at Cowes, Henley, and Lord's at the Eton and Harrow match. None can claim to have preserved the wall of exclusiveness against overpopularity. Only Ascot has maintained its traditions. This does not mean that the public are excluded. If our stranger-friend has any doubts on this score, a walk across the Heath will set his mind at rest. Here is democracy in its fullest sense. From champagne to jellied eels: from strawberries and cream, pretty faces and velvety lawns to ice-cream bricks, lemonade by the gallon, and colloquial breeziness. All contribute to a day graced by the pageantry of the Royal Procession

Pioneers in 1907 ... the ladies crew of the Furnivall Rowing Club bring in their boat.

when the Queen and members of the Royal Family with their guests drive along the course from the Golden Gates into the enclosure behind the Royal Stand. That moment, crowned by the unfurling of the Royal Standard from the mast over the Royal Box, spans the centuries since the days of Queen Anne and Dean Swift.

Cricket I have already commented upon. It requires an English setting to come to life, although at times only an enthusiastic Englishman could swear that life existed. I am not confident of a stranger's reactions. Questions can be disquietening. How can a non-believer be convinced that this slow-moving epic may last for three days? How can he be convinced that half-dozing spectators have the time and inclination to wait for the bitter end? An appreciator of American football may be forgiven if time drags with leaden feet. Tradition may be an additional bait, but we tend to forget that Lord's, Old Trafford, the Oval, and many famous county grounds are only sacred in the eyes of those who know what has taken place on the velvety turf. To the stranger the ground looks commonplace, whilst the surroundings are far from picturesque, yet to the cricket collector any historic item linked with these names is to be treasured.

To convince our stranger that cricket is an inherent part of the English tradition, I would steer clear of county grounds and introduce him to village fare. Here you get the lusty, bread-and-cheese-cum-tankard variety. The turf is bumpy, there is plenty of action, wickets fall quickly, whilst the background is similar to the description by Miss Mitford in *Our Village*, written over a century ago.

For fast-moving sport, football is indicated. The Association code is probably safer in that a novice can follow more easily what is happening, but burning patriotism at its illogical best can only be seen in South Wales during a Rugby International. Why it needs a piece of inflated leather to rouse Welsh blood to fever-pitch is a point that merits psychological examination. Even ignorance of the finer points of play would not spoil a stranger's enjoyment. Such is the vigour and speed of movement between these thirty players that at times the ball is hardly necessary. Opinions vary as to the match of the year. Many will name the Calcutta match at Murrayfield between Scotland and England. My choice would be the Oxford and Cambridge University match at Twickenham, where for two hours the 'other place' is thoroughly hated. But without doubt the game of the people is Association Football. Total attendance at League matches on a Saturday shows that soccer is the national sport, though to conservative minds it lacks the vintage background of the willow.

If deep-rooted tradition is wanted, a visit to the shrine of golf is the answer. St Andrews is the place. Not only is it the ecclesiastical capital of Scotland, richly steeped in historical associations, it is also the spiritual home of golf wherever the game is played. Golf was being played over the stretch of natural golfing country known as the Old Course long before America was thought of. An Act dated 1491 was issued at the command of James IV strictly forbidding the playing of 'Fute-ball, Golfe or uther sik unprofitabill sportis' that were calculated to interfere with 'the commoun gude of the realme and defence thereof'. An even earlier Act of Parliament referring to golf is dated 6 March 1457. So, when the Walker and Ryder Cups are won by the United States of America, we can take comfort in the thought that we must have been extremely successful tutors.

Newmarket Heath, that has seen so much history since the mysterious Devil's Dyke came into being, still retains its racing traditions.

It is impossible to comment on every English sport. No word has been written on the glories of Wimbledon and the growing popularity of lawn tennis. Pages could be penned on the chase, with the challenging note of a hound, the melodious cry of the pack. Then there is the indolent appeal of Henley with its colour and gaiety. The inherent appeal of fishing-rods and guns, thoughts of the Twelfth, with the confusion of Euston before the metropolis is exchanged for the bog stream and glen. To these must be added the placidity of fishing with memories of the Dovey and the Itchen.

Sporting pastimes are not the possession of any one country. Most of the games mentioned are now almost universal. The discerning onlooker, however, will find that by studying the traditional sports of this country, a composite picture gradually emerges of the many-sided facets of our national character, the vision of England that has quietly survived the centuries. Visual reminders confirm this belief, items of sporting interest that are keenly sought by collectors on both sides of the Atlantic. Such a collection becomes a cavalcade of sport stretching over two centuries.

This book is not meant to be a technical discourse. It is written for the enthusiastic collector, the general reader who is attracted by the

memorabilia of sport, often unsophisticated pieces that reflect nineteenth-century events as well as identifiable figures and items commemorating historic sporting occasions, all seen through the eyes of contemporary onlookers. The choice of illustrations presented its own problems. It would have been easy to use only rarities, choice examples associated with museums, London and New York sale rooms, or exclusive antique shops. They would have made a brave showing and whetted appetites, but such tastes are expensive and not everybody can afford exorbitant prices. Not only that but it is discouraging for the beginner-collector to find no reference anywhere to a figure or item he has bought. Probably it was cheap, and more than likely very ordinary, a fact he will realise later, but for the moment it is a 'find'. He wants more information. To repair this annoying omission, I have included some items that can be found in the general run of antique shops. In that sense, they are 'common', but have an equal right to representation alongside the many rare items. Both types are in the native stream of sporting tradition, having its own appeal.

Any genuine collector can look at his pieces and echo Charles Surface's remarks when he entered his picture room, 'You see what a domestic character I am; here I sit of an evening surrounded by my family.' I know the feeling. The commemorative figures and objects are not of my family, though I most certainly could not be fonder of them if they were, but like Charles's great-uncles and aunts, they belong to a bygone age. They are dust 'and their good swords are rust', but the fame of many of them survives and always will.

To speak so may be childish but none the worse for that. It is a gentle, sentimental affection that brings back all manner of memories. It is the essence of true collecting. As Charles Surface said with a bow to his ancestors, 'Gentlemen, your most obedient and very grateful servant.'

(*opposite*): The Newmarket Town Plate founded by Charles II in 1665 and twice won by him, is run over four miles every October.

CHAPTER 2

MEMORABILIA OF HORSERACING

Horse-racing enthusiasts have a rich choice of ephemera. The range is wide: items that can be bought at auction and others so often found unexpectedly in market and mart. An ideal way to assess visually the potential possibilities is to visit the National Horseracing Museum in Newmarket. It has not been opened long. The official ceremony was performed by the Queen in 1983, a gracious gesture of acknowledgment of the immense work put in by David Swannell, one-time senior handicapper of the Jockey Club. The museum is his brain-child, a development of the modest racing museum he laid out in the County Stand at York racecourse. The enormous success of the Derby 200 Exhibition at the Royal Academy of Arts in London gave him the idea of forming a permanent national museum. Such ambitious dreams need a base and lots of money. Newmarket was a natural choice as headquarters of the sport. A Tote building on the Rowley Mile Silver Ring was suggested, but declined because of the difficulties of ensuring security. In 1981 the Jockey Club offered the old Subscription Rooms in the High Street. The site was first-class, the associations right, the Regency interior ideal; the only snag was the price of £500,000. The committee headed by Lord Howard de Walden, the Marquis of Tavistock, Lord Halifax, Robert Fellowes and David Sieff enlisted the help of such wealthy patrons as Paul Mellon, Sir Michael Sobell, Sheikh Mohammed Al Maktoum and Prince Khaled Abdullah, and in a short time the museum became reality. Five display areas display a cross-section of memorabilia, sufficient to whet the appetite of any potential collector. I must mention that certain of the items described were on loan and could be withdrawn from time to time to make way for other items of equal interest on special exhibition. The overall effect is still as pleasing.

In the weighing-room are old scales from Gosforth Park complete with the brass weights from Bath ranging from 11 lb to 56 lb. There are cuff-links, boots, even a nightshirt belonging to Fred Archer. Crude veterinary equipment shows how times have changed. Old clipping shears, rudimentary castration shears, horse spectacles designed by James Beest, and an early nineteenth-century vet's notebook. There are several whips, and silks from owners like Charles Englehard, Paul Mellon and Lord Howard de Walden. The library has a complete collection of Racing Calendars as well as the complete Jockey Club archives. Of particular interest are the hooves of St Simon, unbeaten in any race, now mounted in gold, whilst the hoof of his sire, Galopin, 1875 Derby winner, becomes a part of a silver snuff container. On loan from the Jockey Club is the famous painting of Eclipse by George Stubbs, whilst the Royal College of Veterinary Surgeons has lent the skeleton of this unbeaten horse. When Sir Theodore Cook was gathering material for writing about this near-legendary horse, he asked for any Eclipse relics. He was offered nineteen hooves all guaranteed to be genuine, six skeletons and two skins. At least we know that the Jockey Club does possess a genuine Eclipse hoof mounted on a piece of plate and presented to the Club by William IV. There are innumerable other items of racing memorabilia in the museum including the stuffed head of Persimmon, bred and owned by the Prince of Wales and winner of the 1896 Derby and St Leger. Other royal links come from the contents of Sandringham which were given by the Queen and the Queen Mother, as well as paintings and bronzes from Buckingham Palace and Windsor.

Anyone who is thinking of making a horse-racing collection of Turf memorabilia should visit this Newmarket museum. It is an education in racing lore. As a start attention can be paid to ceramics. Copeland & Garrett produced a white earthenware plate printed in green underglaze in 1847 showing the Main Stand at Epsom. A rare collector's piece is a white earthenware commemorative jug with black transfer pattern showing Fred Archer. A handsome dish commemorates Mahmoud with Charlie Smirke up, whilst Gladiateur features on a mug. Spode produced the first St Leger Plate marking the 1970 St Leger when England's oldest classic was won by Nijinsky with Lester Piggott up. The margin: one length in 3 minutes 6·4 seconds. Owner: Charles W. Engelhard; trainer: Vincent O'Brien.

The John Johnson Collection in the Bodleian Library, Oxford has several items of racing ephemera. Music covers frequently popularised

national events and sporting occasions. A typical example is *The Derby Lancers* alongside *The Derby Stakes* playbill dated 1881 and a Racing Office Poster of 1848. This particular office was in the Strand and advertised sweepstake tickets for the 1849 season and betting lists for all the races. The decorative Music Covers reflect the life of Victorian times. It was an age of live entertainment from musical soirées in middle-class parlours to exuberant acts in taverns and music halls. Sheet music of every description was in demand ranging from bawdy songs to sentimental ballads, a cross-section of dandies to workhouse inmates, of doubtful taste with occasional superb examples of hand-lithography. Many sporting activities were treated. Horseracing was a favourite. As a group they recapture something of the salty atmosphere of those occasions in pungent scenes and vignettes. More tranquil is the *Rotten Row Galop* for the 'pianoforte, composed by Julius Wittenberg'. Rotten Row originated from the French *Route Du Roi* and was opened to the public by Charles II in 1660; on this cover the unknown artist depicts Victorian high society as it was in 1853 when the piece was first published, with families riding in Hyde Park in all their finery. *The Times Galop* of the same date anticipated modern advertising. The copywriter reproduced *The Times* front-page of classified advertisements in which the music title is listed. It was a hard sell with a wide range of musical titles superimposed across the printed page showing the familiar *Times* headline format dated 22 December 1853, price 3/-, with the word *Galop* in large type across the copy. It was a sophisticated advertising technique that must have received editorial approval.

Posters are other examples of social and sporting history being preserved in ebullient fashion. The Victoria and Albert has several examples. E.A. Cox had a London Transport poster in the series London Characters of 1920 showing *The Race Goer*, a bookmaker in unmistakable garb against a racing background. The Kentucky Poster of 1949 by E. McKnight Kauffer is in contrast to Hardy's poster for the 1919 Peace Derby, the first one held at Epsom after its stay at Newmarket for World War I. The Johnson Collection also has a Stud Advertisement dated 1830. In 1824 Squire Thornhill retired his famous horse Emilius to stud at Riddlesworth, near Thetford in Norfolk, where he sired two

(*opposite*): Staffordshire figure of Fred Archer, a natural horseman whose phenomenal success and strong personality captured the public imagination.

Derby winners, Priam and Plenipotentiary, with a stud fee of twelve guineas, and ten shillings and sixpence for the groom. There is a Motor Coach excursion bill dated 1927 recommending the advantages of using a carriage-stand as opposed to the congested Grandstand.

Liberty's of London used to produce an attractive silk-screen scarf depicting famous horses. The issue ceased to be made about the 1960s and are now collector's pieces. In 1952 a scarf was marketed by Welch, Margetson & Co of London showing Tulyar with Charlie Smirke in the saddle. This well-proportioned brown horse combined quality and power to a remarkable degree as Juliet McLeod caught in her action study. Equally effective are the scarves showing Hermit, bought by Captain Machell for 1000 guineas in 1865. After an illustrious career he was retired to stud where his fee was a modest one of 20 guineas. He sired two Derby winners, Shotover and St Blaise, and two Oaks winners, Thebais and Lonely. One of these scarves is in the Victoria and Albert Museum. Minoru, the third and last Derby winner owned by King Edward VII, also features on a scarf. As a four-year-old, the horse was exported to Russia and disappeared during the Russian Revolution. It is said that Minoru along with another famous horse, Aboyeur, who had been sold to the Imperial Racing Club of St Petersburg for £13,000, were harnessed together to a cart and driven from Moscow to Novorossiysk, later being evacuated with the British Military Mission and sent to Siberia, where they died. The scarf is an historic reminder of that time. Sansovino, a strong bay bred and owned by the 17th Earl of Derby and trained by George Lambton, is featured on a scarf, likewise the 6th Earl of Rosebery's classic horse, Blue Peter, which possessed such a flawless action. Scarves such as these are very collectable. Suitably framed, they look right and have historic value.

Whilst visiting the Victoria and Albert Museum it is worth asking to examine three letters from J.F. Herring to W.P. Frith. In Herring's letter dated 18 December 1857, he offers to help Frith with the painting of horses and later gives him several sketches with some pertinent footnotes and rough sketches. The British Museum has a sheet of further Herring drawings of horses for the same purpose. Frith acknowledged the fact that 'I am indebted to Herring, one of the best painters of the racehorse I have ever known, for great assistance in the very small share the high mettled racer has in my work.'

The Stewards of the Jockey Club have many unusual relics. These

The Derby Tankard commemorating the first Derby run on Epsom Downs on 4 May 1780. The race was named after the 12th Earl of Derby.

include the breeches worn by Sam Arnull while riding Diomed in 1780. Unbeaten as a three-year-old, but disappointing at stud in this country, Diomed's fee dropped as low as two guineas when he was sold for export to Virginia in 1798 at the age of twenty-one. The price was fifty guineas. In America Diomed was more successful and founded a potent dynasty that produced Lexington, the greatest sire ever to stand in North America, heading the sires of winners sixteen times, fourteen times in succession. Arnull's breeches recall the description by 'The Druid' of jockey's garb in the eighteenth century: 'brown breeches with bunches of ties which might have made them pass muster for *The Driving Club*, white stockings and short garters'. Another exhibit is the tail of Gladiateur, the chestnut colt owned by Lord Wilton in 1833. Innumerable items associated with famous jockeys come on the market from time to time. The danger of faking is ever-present, particularly with Fred Archer relics. Spurs are obvious because they were an integral part of a jockey's kit in the nineteenth century but rarely identifiable. Archer's racing saddle is in the Queen's collection. Today there is a demand for equipment used by such jockeys as Gordon Richards, Steve Donoghue and Lester Piggott.

Collectors who are prepared to pay high prices might turn to bronzes. They are not everybody's taste, possibly because there is an enormous amount of confused thinking about art, but in no branch of it more than sculpture. Many sculptors have to suffer the criticisms of the totally incompetent. Art seems to attract vague and inconclusive writing, whilst enthusiasm is often clouded by a spate of so-called technical jargon. It is significant that there are so few sculptors today compared with painters. The reason is mainly economic. A painter can complete a painting within weeks, maybe days. A sculptor may take months, perhaps years, to complete a work that has involved heavy outlay in materials without any guarantee of a ready sale. A consequence of this situation is that little is known about sculpture. Critics with more or less sound judgement in painting tend to express opinions on sculpture that are not worth reading, this ignorance being largely due to the paucity of opportunity for study. Satisfactory horse bronzes are rare. Many are motiveless echoes of other echoes, but occasionally these dark bronzes become disconcertingly alive with dynamic intensity and vigorous weight. There is tremendous scope for a sculptor who can tackle this subject with sensitive thought and technical mastery, who can take from the metal, without doing any violence to its nature, a portrayal of its subject, built, in large measure, on the achievement of light and shade. It is interesting to compare the way sculptors of different centuries have modelled the horse. The four gold horses of Chios, surely the most venerable and proudest on earth, were created by the Greek sculptor Lysippus about 300 years before Christ. Standing upon the gallery of San Marco in Venice, it is difficult to imagine that these proud animals stepping forward with arched necks, once decorated the Imperial Box, the Kathisma, of Theodosius III from which the Emperor and Empress watched the chariot races. Miraculously, the four horses escaped when the Christians of the Fourth Crusade sacked Christian Constantinople. Instead of being melted down, they were loaded in the galley of Morosini and taken to Venice where they were placed among the stone lions outside the Arsenal, until, by a stroke of genius, they were set above the west door of St Mark's. One other example of the treatment of equestrian statues, that of Marcus Aurelius in the Piazza del Campidoglio, Rome, designed by Michelangelo. Dated about AD 173, the bronze horse was taken from the Lateran, after being there for 500 years, and set on a base carved from a column of the Temple of Castor and Pollux.

In miniature it is interesting to compare the work of Sir Joseph

Boehm, the Royal Academician, in his bronze study of Favonius now in the possession of the Jockey Club Stewards. This horse won four of the five classics in 1871 for Baron Meyer de Rothschild. The treatment of this big chestnut is pleasing to the eye; the slightly uneven finish infuses life into the model, noting where these small planes begin and end, gives the head a proud air. The Queen has a beautiful Fabergé silver model of Persimmon on an onyx base that marked the Prince of Wales Derby win of 1896. There is a companion consolation figure of St Frusquin, the odds-on favourite for that classic who failed by a neck. Leopold de Rothschild's wife commissioned a similar Fabergé silver model. Another fine bronze is that of Coronach being led in by the Hon. Mrs Macdonald-Buchanan, whilst the Earl of Derby's bronze of Hyperion, known as the outstanding 'little' horse of the twentieth century, does full justice to the claim.

Figures such as these are in a class of their own, but periodically a choice bronze comes on the market. Prices are high, but expected. Almost as satisfying and less expensive are the Royal Worcester race-

Nijinsky, the handsome bay horse by Northern Dancer, owned by Charles Engelhard and trained by Vincent O'Brien, won the Triple Crown in 1970.

horse models, in particular those by Doris Lindner. She was born at Llanyre, Radnorshire in South Wales, studied sculpture at St Martin's School of Art in London, the British Academy in Rome and at Calderon's Animal School in London. Her first models for Royal Worcester were a series of dog portraits and studies of a fox and hound. These were completed in 1931. Her next commission was a series of now famous equestrian models which include *Cantering to the Post* and *Polo Player*. In 1947 the Queen requested that Miss Lindner model Princess Elizabeth in the uniform of Colonel-in-Chief of the Grenadier Guards riding Tommy. This, perhaps her most famous model, set a new style and scale for her work and developed a remarkable precision of detail achieved only by painstaking study of the subject. Doris Lindner died in 1979 but she left a rare collection of fine studies that reflected her love and knowledge of horses. Listing but a few there was *Grundy and Pat Eddery*, first appeared in March 1977, an edition of 500; *Hyperion*, first appeared 1965, edition of 500; *Nijinsky*, first appeared May 1972, edition of 500; *Mill Reef*, first appeared July 1975, edition of 500; *Arkle*, first appeared 1967, edition of 500; *Red Rum*, first appeared July 1975, edition of 250; and *The Winner Braun Horse*, first appeared 1959, an open edition. Royal Worcester can also offer examples of the work of Bernard Winskill, whose deep love of horses is shown in *Minstrel with Piggott* that first appeared in February 1979 with an edition of 150; *At the Start No. 6* first appeared February 1978, an edition of 100; and *Cheltenham*, first appeared February 1979, edition of 100. Any of these fine models enhance a collection.

Sporting pictures, like bronzes, are expensive but desirable. The former covers such a wide range of artist and treatment that choice is difficult. So few painters are in sympathy with the true movement of a horse. Not many have a true working assessment of the animal's anatomy or the rider's role with the result that many pictures have obvious technical faults. Even if the artist has this knowledge and skill, the chances are the landscape may set problems. George Stubbs and Ben Marshall had this difficulty and occasionally sought the aid of other painters to compose their landscapes. Given the resources of a Paul Mellon your gallery would include examples of John Frederick Herring, who had commissions from George IV, William IV, and Queen Victoria; Ben Marshall; James Pollard; George Stubbs, the master of detailed perfection; the Alken family; Emil Adam, whose horses tended to be too

Grundy and Pat Eddery, winner of the King George VI and Queen Elizabeth Diamond Stakes after one of the finest races on record.

static; John Sartorius of prolific talent; Abraham Cooper, who learnt much of his craft from Ben Marshall; Isaac Cullin, whose pseudonym was 'Pantaloon'; Edgar Degas with a passion for sharp detail in behind-the-scenes racing vignettes; Lionel Edwards, whose work was echoed by Peter Biegel; the humorous treatment of sporting subjects by Cecil Aldin; the prolific efforts of Lynwood Palmer; John Wootton, who was responsible for a fresh concept of sporting art; and Sir Alfred Munnings, who became the first sporting President of the Royal Academy. His work, which is delightful, is the spontaneous expression of his personality and captured the atmosphere of the racecourse.

If such paintings are out of reach, less costly is the extensive range of prints. A signed Munnings print of Brown Jack or Humorist with Steve Donoghue up may be second best, but, along with others, give considerable pleasure. Often overlooked are the coloured caricature prints of the eighteenth and early nineteenth century, whilst few collectors look for original caricature drawings, in pen or pencil or watercolour, of that period. The caricature offers a rewarding by-path. Thomas Rowlandson's drawings exist today in large numbers. They vary in quality and value, whilst forgeries are about. He was always drawing, usually in pen and watercolour, but also in pen only, and sometimes in pencil. He was ebullient, sometimes cruel, and generally viewed his fellow-creatures, particularly on the racecourse, with a boisterous and vulgar good humour. His satire was mainly social. Occasionally it is possible to find a bargain once you can distinguish between a real Rowlandson and a fake.

CHAPTER 3

ENGLAND'S LAST FOLK ART

Staffordshire pottery figures are England's last folk art. As a group they form an unsophisticated frieze of eighteenth- and nineteenth-century customs, events and activities, including identifiable figures, remembered by incidents, historic or notorious, all shaped by contemporary potters. Cricket is no exception, though the range is somewhat narrow. There is George Parr, known as 'The Lion of the North'. Born at Radcliffe-on-Trent on 22 May 1826, Parr played his first match for Nottinghamshire on 16 June 1845 and continued a cricketing career until 1871. Without the inhibiting distraction of leg-theory bowling, Parr was famed for leg hits, often out of the ground, the ball frequently landing in the branches of an elm almost in line with square-leg. By the mid-nineteenth century it became known as George Parr's tree. When he died in 1891 a branch was fashioned into a wreath and placed on his grave. The sports equipment manufacturers, Gunn and Moore, shaped a bat from wood taken from the tree which is now in the Long Room at Lord's. In 1978 the Nottinghamshire County Club marketed some miniature bats, $11\frac{1}{2}$ ins long, made from this elm and bearing an outline of the tree in full leaf with the inscription *Parr's Tree*, plus biographical details.

Parr was one of the key players in the renowned All England X1. He scored a century on his first appearance at Leicester in 1847, followed by innings of 78 and 64 against sides that fielded 18 men. When William Clarke died in 1856, he became manager of the All England XI and was made Nottinghamshire captain in the same year. He skippered the All England XI of professionals in 1859 for a five-match series in Canada and America. They were undefeated with one game played in a snow-storm. In 1865 he captained the second team to tour Australia. Unlike H.H. Stephenson's team which lost twice, Parr's men were never beaten. The George Parr figure, $13\frac{1}{2}$ ins high, shows him holding a ball in the right hand with a bat leaning against the stumps, the traditional way of indicating captaincy. The player is bearded, wears a sprigged shirt and sash, with the regulation cap worn at that time. The colouring is tasteful.

A companion figure, also untitled, is usually identified as Julius Caesar, the hard-hitting Surrey batsman who played for Clarke's All England XI from 1849 to 1857, then served under Parr's captaincy until 1867. The 14 ins figure has a sprigged shirt and sash similar to Parr's, but favours a more conventional cap and has taken guard in a somewhat unprofessional manner. Not a great deal is known about Caesar, except that he was short. Contemporary potters were not unduly concerned about accuracy of detail, but extremes of height were usually recorded. After studying and comparing prints, it is possible that the figure could be Joseph Guy, a young Nottinghamshire batsman, born in 1814, who was in the 1847 All England XI. Clarke's description was apt; 'Joe Guy, sir, all ease and elegance, fit to play before Her Majesty in a drawing-room.' When not playing cricket, Guy was a baker, later becoming an inn-keeper at the *Roebuck* in Mansfield Road, Nottingham. Joseph Guy was the type to appeal to the potter's skill. There are smaller versions of both figures, $10\frac{1}{2}$ ins high, with similar markings. Modern reproductions are now on the market, but are easily recognisable by indifferent modelling and harsh colouring.

Three collectable figures were made of cricketers who were legends in their lifetime. Fuller Pilch (1803–1870) began his career as a batsman for Norfolk, then switched to Bury before joining Kent at a wage of £100 a year. The move was successful. He stayed from 1836 until his death in 1870, though his playing career ended in 1854. Skill with the bat made him Champion of England from 1833, when he thrashed Tom Marsden of Sheffield in a single-wicket match. His highest score of 160 was taken off the bowling of William Lillywhite in 1837. Between 1827 and 1849 Pilch played in twenty-four Gentlemen versus Players matches and was one of the stars in Clarke's All England XI of 1847. Technically Pilch was the first to develop forward play using a short-handled bat and an upright stance. The model is $7\frac{1}{2}$ ins high, untitled,

(*opposite*): George Parr, leading figure of the famous All England XI. (*overleaf*): Julius Caesar, outstanding batsman who toured with Parr's team in America and Australia.

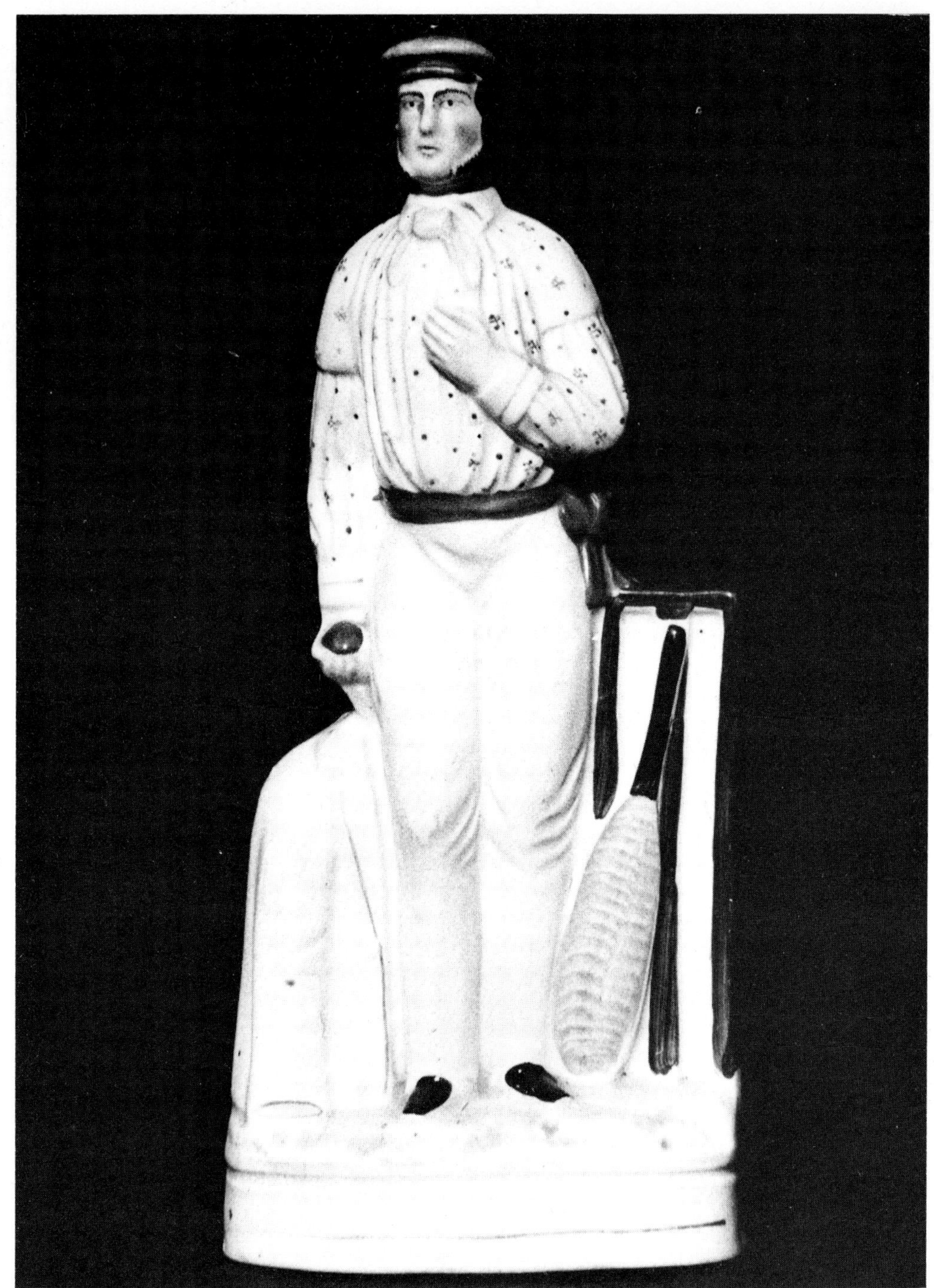

23

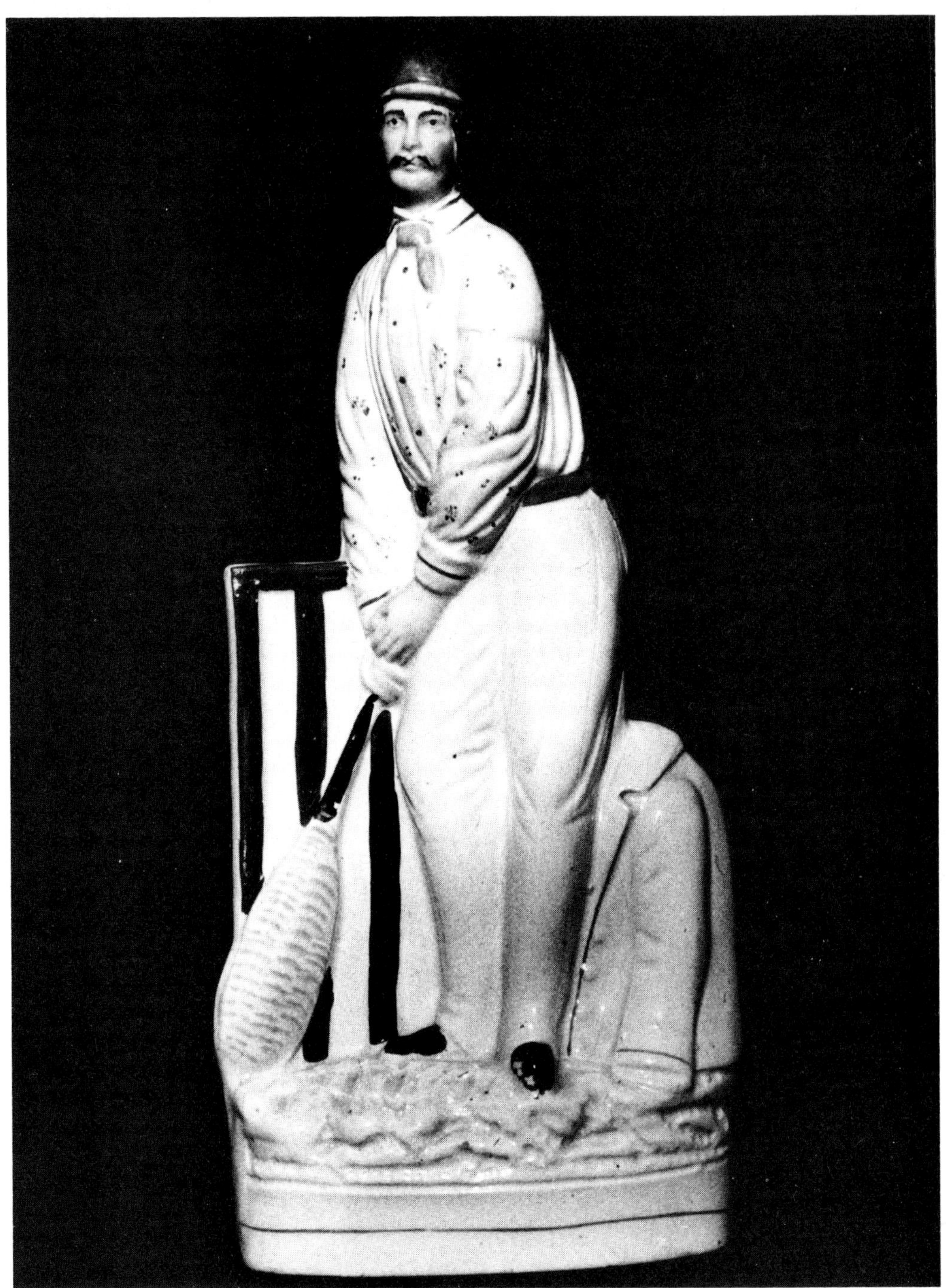

24

and attractively coloured. He wears a top hat, shirt and trousers, holding the bat in front of the wicket. A tree trunk in the background serves as a spill-holder. The date is about 1844.

The wicket-keeper, Tom Box, is the second figure. This Sussex player, born in 1809, had become by 1832 one of the finest keepers in England, his only rivals being the Kentishmen, Jenner and Wenman. The model, $6\frac{1}{2}$ ins high, untitled, of good colouring, wears the traditional top hat and stands behind the wicket with a pronounced open stance against a wooded background with a jacket slung over a branch. The date is about 1844. It is interesting to recall that John Wisden learnt his cricket from Tom Box and lived at his house after Box senior died.

The last figure of the triumvirate is Frederick William Lillywhite, a little man, five feet four inches in height, who played in high Gladstone collar and top hat. According to contemporary critics, he was the best bowler in England, an opinion endorsed by Lillywhite for there was nothing modest about the Victorian ego. Lillywhite introduced guile into the art of bowling. Slow-medium pace, he proved that subtlety could be as devastating as the brute strength of Alfred Mynn. Variation of length on unpredictable wickets took its toll of batsmen. In 1853 Lillywhite, then sixty-three, was given a farewell benefit match. England played Sussex at Lord's. George Parr was in the Sussex side along with Lillywhite's sons, John and James. England included Guy, Clarke, Hillyer, Caffyn and Lockyer. Lillywhite opened the bowling, but after eleven overs was taken ill and had to leave the field. A substitute took his place. England won by 197 runs. Lillywhite lived for another year, then died suddenly on the evening of 20 August 1854. He is buried in Highgate cemetery. The monument erected by the MCC has this inscription:

Lillywhite, born June, 1792 died August 21st, 1854. A man to be remembered as long as The National Game of England, by the practice and tuition of which for years he earned an honest livelihood. Rarely has a man received more applause on his vocation. Few have administered to more happy hours. From an humble station he achieved a world-wide reputation, teaching, both by precept and example, a sport in which the blessings of youthful strength and spirits may be most innocently enjoyed, to the exercise of the mind, the discipline of temper, and the

Fuller Pilch, Thomas Box and Frederick Lillywhite, cricketing figures based on portraits in *Illustrated London News* of 15 and 22 July 1843.

general improvement of the man. This Monument testifies the respect of the noblemen and gentlemen of the Marylebone Cricket Club, and of many private friends, to one who did his duty in that state of life to which it had pleased God to call him.

Even in death distinctions had to be observed. The pottery figure, $6\frac{1}{2}$ ins high, is untitled, probably unnecessary as he was so well known. Like the other two figures, the colouring is good. He is shown facing half-right, a cricket ball in the right hand, and a spill-holder background with a coat hanging from a branch.

Contemporary confirmation is interesting. *The Illustrated London News* published engravings of all the aforementioned three figures. On 22 July 1843 Lillywhite was featured in connection with the match between the All England XI and the Marylebone Club. The bowler was in the

26

England team, whilst Pilch and Box played for the Club. The issue of 15 July 1843 carried the engraved likenesses of Box and Pilch in positions identical with the Staffordshire figures. On this occasion Pilch was in the Kent side against an All England XI that included Lillywhite and Box.

The same characters decorate three Pratt-ware jugs, with one difference. The figure of Lillywhite is inscribed to Wm Clarke, the potter honouring another cricketer with the same mould and infringing his

Rare jug showing William Clarke, one of the all-time greats, and Fuller Pilch, single-wicket match English Champion in 1833.

Realistic action poses based on studies of C.B. Fry.

own copyright. William Clarke was a natural selection for he ranked among the great names in cricket. Few men did more to popularise the game. In 1846 he founded an Eleven of England as a private venture and incurred criticism for trying to gain a monopoly. In many ways Clarke was the forerunner of Kerry Packer. He picked the top-class players and toured the country with an open challenge. It was Victorian professionalism in action. Clarke was the first man to captain Nottinghamshire and remained in charge until the year before his death in 1856. For forty years he exercised enormous influence on the game. His first big match was in 1816, the last in June 1856, when he claimed a wicket for England with his final ball. Ranked as the finest under-arm bowler with a vicious leg-spin, he took 476 wickets in 1853 for an average of 8 runs apiece. William Clarke is a choice addition to any collector's shelf.

There are several smaller pottery figures of batsmen, bowlers and wicketkeepers, all unidentifiable crude attempts to capture the naive spirit of the game. Occasionally the potter had a dual loyalty. Two flgures on a base depict a girl clutching a late Victorian tennis racket, whilst the man has a cricket bat in one hand and a ball in the other. More unusual is the pairing of two officers in uniforms of the Volunteer Rifles carrying cricket bats instead of weapons, like another figure wearing a similar uniform holding a cricket bat with the left hand resting on his waist. Date about 1860, height $11\frac{1}{2}$ ins.

Serious collectors may regard such figures as frivolous, but they are sought after. Rarity value reflected in auction prices prove they are desirable. In a different category the range of bronze cricketing figures has instant appeal. As befits works of art, they are expensive and comparatively rare, but can convey something of the pent-up energy about to be unleashed in this example of a bowler about to deliver a fast 'un. Those who prefer identifiable figures have a limited choice, though C.B. Fry appears in several poses, whilst a modern figure of Geoffrey Boycott by J. Apkins showing the fluency of the Yorkshireman's batting stroke frozen in bronze is a collector's gem.

CHAPTER 4

SPORTING STEVENGRAPHS

In Victorian times, Stevengraphs were sold for a shilling apiece. Today these woven-silk pictures are collector's pieces. They are the result of a Government policy to allow the importation of cheap foreign silk goods, a decision disastrous to Coventry which in 1700 was the centre of a flourishing market for silk ribbons. By 1860 most of the weavers had failed. Thomas Stevens was the exception. After experimenting he introduced new techniques and adapted the Jacquard loom for the production of small multi-coloured pictures. In 1863 he marketed the first woven-silk book-markers. The response was sufficiently encouraging to widen the range to include contemporary scenes and portraits of royalty and leading personalities. In 1879 he produced silk pictures with mounts to give a three-dimensional effect. Large quantities were produced to cope with a strong export order-book, many having French and German titles on their mounts, whilst those for America frequently had the names and addresses of American agents on the back.

It would be difficult and expensive to form a definitive collection as so many were produced, but limiting the search to sporting subjects is a different matter. A complete collection is quite possible and gratifying to those interested in hunting, horseracing, boxing, rowing, coursing, trotting races, Victorian tennis, rugby, baseball, penny-farthing racing, early cricket and even a Spanish bullfight – enough to satisfy any specialist.

Are You Ready is a delightful study of the start of the Oxford and Cambridge Boat Race on the Thames. It was registered on 8 January 1880 and shows in the background that public interest in the event had attracted a flotilla of spectator craft possibly stimulated by the controversial dead-heat of 1877. 'Honest John' Phelps, the waterman who had judged the race for years, was felt by many to have made a mistake.

In 1879 neither of the crews were of particularly high standard, with Cambridge the weaker. The Oxford president, W.H. Grenfell later Lord Desborough did not row himself, and only Southwell of the 1878 Dark Blues crew remained.

Oxford won the toss and chose the Surrey station. Cambridge were very fast starters and cleared their opponents in about a minute and a half. Rowing the slower stroke, they went on gaining and were some three lengths ahead at Hammersmith. Nasty water in Corney Reach helped Oxford to close the gap, but smoother water round Barnes suited Cambridge who won by three lengths in 21 min 18 sec. W.H. Grenfell is the subject of a *Spy* cartoon entitled 'Taplow Court'.

The Final Spurt is the companion silk and makes an attractive pairing. It is interesting to note that the crews are rowing in the opposite direction from that at the start.

The Last Lap applies to two variations of the same subject. The earlier silk shows five riders garbed in jockey-style colours and caps taking part in a penny-farthing race watched by a crowd lining a rail with an indicator-structure in the centre. The date when the title was first listed was 31 October 1879. The later version shows five competitors on conventional bicycles racing, like the Boat Race silk, in the opposite direction. The men are dressed in shorts. Behind the lined spectators is an impressive grandstand, whilst the industrial skyline of Coventry is in the background, an appropriate touch for the city used to be the hub of the bicycle industry. The Recreation Ground had an official racing track. This later Stevengraph is very rare. The silk has twelve colours.

The First Touch shows a rugby match in progress with a player about to score a try. All the men wear breeches and caps, whilst the referee is dressed in a town suit and hat. Crowd attendance looks healthy. The colours of blue, yellow, and scarlet are vivid. Date about 1881.

Another sporting Victorian scene is *The First Over*. It shows an early cricket match with a bowler making an under-arm delivery. The umpire is top-hatted with the fieldsmen shown in poses of anticipation. The batsman looks set for a quick single. As a variation to the usual line of spectators, some are sitting on the grass by the boundary. This is one of the earliest of sporting Stevengraphs and dates from May 1880.

The First Innings does not refer to cricket but depicts an American baseball match. Detail is good, players animated, and spectators are in the foreground. The silk is rare. *The Home Stretch* is another unusual silk showing an American trotting match between two entrants. The detail is excellent and catches the tension of the moment. Entirely different is the *Spanish Bull Fight* though the ring looks somewhat crowded with onlookers and an irate bull within yards. The colours are good with close attention to detail. Date about 1898 and rare. More tranquil is *The First Set* showing a Victorian mixed-doubles tennis match, with the players and spectators in the clothes of that period – by today's standard somewhat over-clothed. Date about 1881 and rare.

A set of fox-hunting scenes begins with *The Meet*, first registered on 26 January 1880, and makes a pleasing landscape view. *Full Cry* shows the huntsmen and huntswomen with the hounds and fox in full flight across the countryside culminating in *The Death* with the huntsmen and hounds grouped round the unfortunate fox. Of the set, the third is the rarest, whilst *Full Cry* can also be found with the title in German, *Jagdgeschrei* and French, *La Chasse*.

The Start shows the start of a race between seven horses, issued on 15 December 1879 and companion to *The Struggle*, later renamed *The Finish*. A landscape steeplechase silk, *The Water Jump*, was issued about 1881, again showing seven horses negotiating a hazard. A particularly fine silk – according to some experts the finest of all Stevengraphs – shows an action study of the racehorse *Iroquois* with Fred Archer in the saddle. This combination produced in 1881 the first American Derby winner for his owner Pierre Lorillard, a tobacco millionaire. In 1879 he had sent some yearlings to Newmarket with his trainer Jacob Pincus, among them Iroquois. Pincus' training methods were viewed with scepticism by more conservative-minded stables. Anyone who worked his horses on the clock was suspect. Results proved otherwise. Iroquois, a handsome horse with a fluid action, was bred by Aristides Welsh at Erdenheim Stud near Philadelphia and was by Leamington out of Maggie B.B., by Australian. He ran twelve times as a two-year-old and won four races, including the Chesterfield Stakes at Newmarket and the Lavant Stakes at Goodwood. He began his three-year-old stint by finishing second to the Duke of Westminster's Peregrine in the Two Thousand Guineas, a promising performance considering the horse was not completely fit. Fred Archer was impressed and asked Pincus if he could have the ride on Iroquois in the Derby. He started as a strongly backed second favourite at 11–2.

That Derby Day was one of the hottest on record. In the early stages the field of fifteen was led by Lord Rosebery's Voluptuary, who three years later was to win the Grand National Steeplechase. With two furlongs to go Voluptuary weakened. Scobell went to the front followed by Town Moor and Cumberland with Peregrine in close contention. His jockey used the whip and Peregrine, who was on the rails, swerved to the right, leaving a gap that Archer was quick to take. Iroquois closed on Peregrine. In the final furlong he won by a neck, with Town Moor third, two lengths behind Peregrine, and Scobell fourth. The victory was popular. Lorillard had not made the trip, but his wife was present with a large American party. In New York, dealings on Wall Street were temporarily suspended, whilst thousands of Irish-Americans celebrated the victory as an English setback. Not until 1954 was there another American Derby win, the second being that of Never Say Die.

This Stevengraph has two variations. In one Archer's cap is black with his sleeves red and black; the other has a white cap with black and white sleeves. Both are rare.

Another landscape view is *The Slip*, a coursing picture showing two dogs just released by the slipper while the judge, on horseback, is about to follow to note the dog's progress after the hare. *The Slip* is the pair to this silk and shows the judge awarding the first point. The slipper is depicted in red standing alongside the beaters. There is a variation that omits the slipper. The date is 1887.

Apart from the pictorial scenes, Thomas Stevens also issued a number of sporting portrait silks. The study *W.G. Grace* which shows the player at the wicket is referred to in Chapter 7. In spite of being produced in large quantities in 1896, it is extremely rare. In horse-racing the portrait of Fred Archer was the most popular and the first of the sporting likenesses. He is shown wearing the silks of many of the top owners of that time. As a guide these are the main colours:

LORD FALMOUTH: black body to jacket, white sleeves, red cap.
MR MANTON (pseudonym for the Duchess of Montrose);
    scarlet jacket and cap.
DUKE OF WESTMINSTER: primrose jacket, black cap.
'MR PECK': blue body, orange sleeves, black cap.
PRINCE OF WALES: blue body, scarlet sleeves, black cap.
MR T. JENNINGS: silver grey jacket, black cap – or – silver grey
    jacket and cap with primrose sleeves.

F. BARRETT.

silk with mauve jacket and black cap.
CAPT. CHRISTIE: silks all cream.

Apart from these, there are *Archer* Stevengraphs showing the jockey in the colours of unrecorded owners, with the occasional variation that Fred Archer's signature does not appear at the lower right hand corner.

There are four more jockey portraits. *C. Wood* was produced in the silks of three owners: with Mr Peck's colours of blue jacket with orange sleeves and blue cap; with Captain Christie's or General Wood's colours of cream jacket, sleeves and cap; and an unidentified owner who raced with colours of yellow jacket with blue sleeves and cap. The title was first listed in 1887.

Fred Barrett was an extremely popular Stevengraph. This farmer's son was one of the top Victorian jockeys, principally engaged by the Duke of Portland. In 1889 he set up a new record of stake-money on one horse by winning £34,616 on Donovan. He had difficulty in making the weight and died in 1895 aged twenty-eight. The portrait was first listed in 1893 in which the jockey wears the colours of Mr R. Martin, white jacket with black sleeves and cap. *John Osborne* is a very rare portrait. Full-face, he is shown in Prince Soltykoff's colours of deep rose jacket with black sash, rose sleeves and cap, also in the colours of either Sir Green Price or Mr R.C. Vuners, of violet jacket with white sash, violet sleeves and cap. The date is 1887.

Tom Cannon is a handsome portrait, though Stevens has strengthened what was a delicate-looking man with the lightest touch. Not for him the harsher handling of many of his contemporaries. His gentler approach was evident in the way he tackled two-year-olds and fillies. Cannon won the Derby once and the Two Thousand Guineas twice on fillies. His riding tactics were like those of Harry Wragg of a later generation. He preferred to hold back for a calculated late challenge. Although reserved by nature, his background was tough, with a father who was a horse-dealer in Windsor. Tom Cannon was born at Eton on 23 April 1846. His first mount was Mavourneen at the age of fourteen, hardly successful for he fell in the Saltram Handicap at Plymouth in 1860, but registered his first win the same year on Lord Portsmouth's My Uncle. His potential was noted by the Danebury trainer, John Day,

(*opposite*): Fred Barrett, well-known Victorian jockey.

whose daughter Catherine he was to marry. His first classic success was on Repulse in the One Thousand Guineas, followed in 1869 with the Oaks on Brigantine; he went on to become champion jockey in 1872 with eighty-seven winners. Other important wins included the double in the Two Thousand and One Thousand Guineas on Lord Lonsdale's Pilgrimage. For the Duke of Westminster he won the Two Thousand Guineas and the Derby on Shotover in 1882 and the Oaks on Geheimniss for Lord Stamford in the same year. For James Ryan he won the Two Thousand Guineas on Enterprise and Enthusiast in 1887 and 1889. In all Cannon rode 1,544 winners. Eventually he took over the Danebury stable from his father-in-law and was responsible for one of the largest strings in the country. His sons Mornington and Kempton became first-class jockeys. After retiring he acted as Clerk of the Course at Stockbridge, later taking over the Grosvenor Arms in the same town. His daughter, Margaret, married the steeplechase jockey Ernest Piggott, their son Keith being the father of Lester Piggott. There are four Stevengraph variations. Cannon is shown in his own colours of white and scarlet hoops with white cap: Lord Rosebury's colours of rose and primrose hoops with rose cap: H. Crocker's colours of blue jacket and sleeves with gold cap: and Baron de Rothschild's colours of blue and yellow hoops with yellow cap. The signature is not always woven at the base. The portrait was first listed in 1887.

An unusual and very rare Stevengraph shows *R. Howell, Champion of the World*. This moustached gentleman is shown head and shoulders in an athletic-looking vest buttoned up to the neck. At the bottom of the silk a penny-farthing race is taking place in a stadium with a towering grandstand packed with spectators. At the top of the Stevengraph are three examples of early bicycles. The date is 1887, the year in which the Badminton Library published a volume entitled *Cycling*. Comprehensive in its survey, there is no reference in the section on riders to R. Howell. None of the books dealing with this form of exercise of that period cast any light on this gentleman, yet he was sufficiently famous to be named Champion of the World on this Stevengraph. Apart from the laconic title, he must have been exceptionally retiring, though in appearance the features look aggressive.

(*opposite*): This Stevengraph of W.G. Grace at the wicket is very rare. It was produced to mark his century of centuries in 1895.

"W. G."

The Stevengraph collection of sporting subjects is completed with four boxers. *Jem Smith* shows a muscular pugilist. He was born in 1863 and began work in a London timber-yard. His boxing career bridged the years between the old Prize Ring and the Queensberry Rules. If he looks rugged, the image must have been right for a fighter had to be tough to survive. Smith battled with gloves and without, though he really belonged to the bare-knuckle bruisers. In 1885 he claimed the Championship of England after beating Jack Davies for the title and 500 dollars a side. He won this title in a gloved contest in September 1889, when he beat Jack Wannop in 10 rounds, but his toughest Prize-Ring bout was on 19 December 1887 at Isle de Souverains, France when with bare knuckles he went 106 rounds against the American pugilist, Jake Kilrain. The light became so bad that fighting was impossible, and the contest was abandoned after two hours and thirty minutes and declared a draw. In November 1889, Smith was thrashed by the negro boxer, Peter Jackson. July 1891 saw him lose his title to Ted Pritchard in three rounds, he made a comback at the age of thirty-two in 1895, reclaiming the title from Pritchard in five rounds, but a beating by George Crisp in February 1897 ended his fighting career. The Stevengraph was first listed in 1888 with minor variations, Smith's socks being green, yellow or black.

Charlie Mitchell was an even rougher character. Born in Birmingham in 1856, he began his pugilistic career as a lightweight in 1878. Four years later he became middleweight champion of England through winning an open competition at Chelsea. Eight months later he took the heavyweight title the same way. In 1883 he went to America to fight the American champion, John L. Sullivan at the old Madison Square Garden. The Englishman put the American on the floor, the first man ever to do so, but satisfaction was shortlived. Sullivan proceeded to crush the game little fighter who had scaled only 160 lb, and administered such punishment the contest was stopped by the police in the third round. In spite of the thrashing, Mitchell pressed for a return fight. Eventually a match was arranged at Chantilly, France for 10 March 1888. Mitchell still conceded 33 lb and was at a disadvantage in height, reach and power. On the other hand, he was wily. No one could teach him anything about elbowing, gouging, spiking or kneeing. He knew all the tricks. Sullivan wanted to fight on a solid platform. Mitchell insisted on turf which was better for his more agile feet. The Irish-

American plumped for a sixteen-foot ring which would have meant Mitchell standing up and fighting, but the Birmingham bruiser stipulated it had to be a twenty-four footer otherwise he would not sign. Luck was also on the Englishman's side. Heavy rain thirty-six hours before the fight began left the turf soggy which favoured the lighter man.

Because of the legal penalties, the venue was not made public. The date was known to be 10 March and the rumour spread that the site would be near Boulogne. The gendarmes concentrated on that area, whilst the fighters and their supporters went from Calais to Baron Rothschild's estate at Chantilly, a few miles from Paris. The ring was staked out behind the stables whilst forty-one enthusiasts, including reporters and Ann Livingston disguised as a man, waited for the fight to begin. Ann Livingston would have made an ideal subject for a Stevengraph, but possibly the full-blown beauty was too temptestuous for such sober treatment. She had been on the stage as a chorus girl and starred in the revival of an 'allegorical drama' *The Black Crook*, which was America's first leg show. As Sullivan's mistress, she kept well in the background. She went to all his fights disguised as a man, though judging by the picture of her that appeared in the *Police Gazette*, it is difficult to imagine how such curves could be made masculine – but at the ringside such details are an advantage.

Sullivan was the first to enter the ring. He was dressed in white tights, green stockings, black laced boots, with his black hair shorn close and his moustache removed. Mitchell wore white tights, black stockings and black laced boots. The fight was a bare-knuckle affair with thirty-second rests after falls. Sullivan set the pace, but it was six minutes before he could land a blow on Mitchell, who dropped under a right cross. He was not hurt, but part of the strategy was to take as many knock-downs as possible to take advantage of the thirty-second respite. He overdid it in the ninth round by dropping before he had been hit. Sullivan's seconds claimed a foul which the referee disallowed, but he warned Mitchell that if he continued to sham disqualification would follow. In the fifteenth round Sullivan was hit below the belt. Soggy conditions took their toll and both fighters were near exhaustion. Sullivan's right arm was almost useless; Mitchell's left eye was closed. In the thirty-eighth round both men fell to the ground without a blow being exchanged. When they staggered to their feet, a light punch by

Sullivan again put Mitchell on the turf. Conditions were frightful. Incessant rain, the light failing after three hours of battling, they came up for the thirty-ninth round. Appeals were made to the referee to abandon the bout and a draw was announced.

Because of Mitchell's absence in America the English heavyweight title had been declared vacant. In February 1890 Mitchell was matched with Jem Mace for the championship. With Mace fifty-eight years of age, the contest was one-sided and Mitchell won in three rounds. In January 1894 Mitchell was beaten by Jim Corbett, retired from the ring, and died at Brighton in 1918. The Stevengraph shows Mitchell in fighting pose with bare fists, and unlike the depictions of other Victorian boxers no ring is shown in the background. The silk was first listed in 1888.

A third boxer silk is *Jake Kilrain*, an American boxer with a long list of fistic successes, possibly best remembered for being involved in the last bare-knuckle fight staged in America. His opponent on that blazing hot day in 1889, with the temperature reading 103°F in the shade, was the famous John L. Sullivan. The ring was on the estate of Charles Rich, a wealthy lumberman, at Richburg, Mississippi, some 100 miles upriver from New Orleans. Kilrain was first to appear, wearing black tights and blue stockings. Charley Mitchell, who had trained him, and Mike Donovan, former middleweight champion, acted as seconds. Sullivan wore green tights and white stockings, with Muldoon and Cleary as seconds. The fight itself was vicious and full of mixed tactics, Kilrain throwing his opponent to the ground with a cross buttock and being cautioned in the third round for throwing a low punch, a nicety that hardly seemed to matter. In the seventh round Sullivan's ear was torn by a swinging right, but he was encouraged by flooring Kilrain in the eighth. Both men took terrible punishment. Kilrain had been coached by Mitchell to take to the turf as often as possible until Sullivan was exhausted. Unfortunately in the process the challenger was exhausting himself. No man had ever stayed so many rounds with Sullivan, who was proving the fitter man. The sixty-eighth round virtually turned the contest in Sullivan's favour. A right uppercut to the jaw literally lifted Kilrain off the ground. The effects of the blow were evident. Five painful rounds followed. Mitchell kept urging Kilrain to fight. Donovan was fearful that one more blow might be fatal. In the seventy-fifth round Kilrain dropped to a light tap. Mitchell proposed a draw but Sullivan refused. Then, acting on his own initiative, Donovan tossed the sponge into the ring. After two hours and fifteen minutes under heatwave conditions, Sullivan was still champion. Now Jake Kilrain is remembered by a portrait silk that was first listed in 1888.

The final boxing Stevengraph is that of *John L. Sullivan*. In many ways the 'Boston Strong Boy' was idolised by the American public in the same way that Jack Dempsey was a legend. John L. was born of Irish parents in Boston, Massachusetts in October 1858. He challenged the American champion, Paddy Ryan, in 1880, only to be rejected. After that he toured the country offering 50 dollars to anyone who could stay four rounds with him. Later he made a similar tour with a thousand-dollar challenge. In Mississippi City, 7 February 1882, he knocked out Ryan in $10\frac{1}{2}$ minutes of a bare-knuckle contest to take the heavyweight title. In the previous Stevengraphs of Mitchell and Kilrain details have been given of Sullivan's prowess as a fighter, but after 1884 he drank too much and became out of condition. Even so, it was not until September 1892 that he was finally beaten by Jim Corbett, who knocked him out after twenty-one rounds. Prior to this fight John L. had not fought for thirty-eight months, but had been on the stage in a play: 'Honest Hearts and Willing Hands'. In later years Sullivan became a reformed character and lectured on the evils of drinking. He died in his sixtieth year.

The Stevengraph usually carries an outline of his career on the reverse side with a lengthy list of his fights and victories. The account ends in flowery fashion: 'The Champion possesses the agility of a lightweight, while as a clever fighter and a punishing hitter his equal has never been known or heard of. No man has ever been known to deal him an effective blow, and during his career he has never as much as received a discoloured eye. As a pugilist Sullivan is a marvel and during his short career he has raised out of the profession over £30,000.' The title was first listed in 1888.

A collection of sporting Stevengraphs makes a pleasant entity. It reflects a Victorian background when most events were in a formative state, whilst the outstanding personalities were 'characters' in more senses than one. Always be on the look-out for silks in good condition with the colours bright. Ideally the card-mounts should be originals, uncreased and not stained.

CHAPTER 5

COMMEMORATIVE PLATES

Plates commemorating sporting personalities, events and venues offer an excellent field for the collector. As so often happens, cricket gives the widest choice. Outstanding is the one marking W.G. Grace's century of centuries. Blue-printed and gilded, it was issued in 1895 by the Coalport Porcelain Works. An excellent modern version has been produced by Coalport, faithfully following the 1895 design except that the bats, bails and stumps have been redrawn to conform with the design of present-day equipment. The 1983 version has a limited edition of 750.

Another Coalport cricketing plate marked the century of centuries by Sir John Berry Hobbs, 1905–1923, that had a limited production of 500. This peer of batsmen is portrayed head and shoulders in the centre with the statistical record of individual centuries listed in a spoked circle with an encircling frieze of cricket balls and bails. The same treatment was given to John Edrich when he reached the same number of centuries. The centre medallion has a line drawing of Edrich ringed by a garland into which is incorporated the badges of Surrey CCC and England. The plate is finished in Surrey brown and limited to 1500. Colin Cowdrey's feat is similarly honoured with a limited edition of 2500. Geoff Boycott had the satisfaction of reaching one hundred centuries in first-class cricket during a Test Match against Australia and before his own home crowd at Headingley. The line drawing of Boycott has the badges of Yorkshire CCC and England incorporated into the garland of laurel. His distinctive signature is on the back of the plate which has a limited edition of 1500. Quite different is the Coalport plate commemorating the centenary of the first match played in England against Australia in 1880. This took place at Lord's on 28 August 1880. Interlinked circles contain the outlines and cap badges of the two countries. Two segments of the interlocking ribbons graphically illustrate the progress achieved in international travel during the past century. The outline of the screw barque SS *Garonne*, the ship which brought the Australian team over in 1880, is technically factual and taken from a contemporary photograph extracted from the archives of the National Maritime Museum, Greenwich. Its tedious journey of 45 days contrasts vividly with that measured in hours by modern aircraft. The whole is ringed by the usual design of crossed cricket bats interspersed with cricket balls and edged in gold. On the reverse side is depicted the full score card of the 1880 Test played at the Oval. It was the only time that three members of the Grace family played together in a Test. A few days after the match, G.F. Grace contracted an illness on a train journey and died of pneumonia. The edition was limited to 1000 pieces.

The County Championship Plate was first produced to celebrate the 100th Anniversary in 1973 of the inauguration of the County Cricket Championship and the winning of the Championship in that year by Hampshire. It features around the outer rim the badges of the seventeen first-class counties flanked on either side by cricket bats and balls. The bats are further decorated with symbolic blue ribbons and sprigs of willow. The centre medallion consists of a line drawing of the Worcester County ground with the cathedral in the background. This series of commemorative plates is on-going. The champions in 1974 were Worcester, Leicester in 1975, and so on. The Middlesex plate in 1976 was particularly attractive. The rim had the usual border of the seventeen county badges, but the centrepiece featured in sepia tones a line drawing of the Lord's pavilion. The reverse side included the signature of the captain with the badge of the county, the date it was established, and the honours achieved in the Championship up to that date. There was a limited edition of 1500. The 1977 plate marked one of the closest finishes to decide the Championship. At the start of play on the last day of the season any one of three counties could have been the outright winner. In fact it was not until after the tea interval that a decision was reached which left Kent and Middlesex sharing the honours – only the third time this century the Championship has not been won outright. The plate gives equal prominence to Kent and Middlesex with the reverse side containing statistical data and the signatures of the two captains.

Royal Worcester have also published some fine cricketing commemorative plates carrying the signatures of various Test sides.

Much older are the plates carrying the full-length figures of outstanding cricketers of their day. Sydney F. Barnes was understandably featured. His career was remarkable. In first-class cricket he took 653 wickets for an average of 16·93, but the greater part of his career was in League cricket where he claimed some 4000 wickets for an average of less than 7 runs apiece. In the second Test at Melbourne in the 1911–12 tour he took five Australian wickets of Kelleway, Bardsley, Hill, Armstrong and Minnett in eleven overs for 6 runs on a batting wicket. Nine of the overs were maidens.

For the XXI Olympiad at Montreal in 1976 Wedgwood made a special plate. In the traditional Wedgwood blue it has within the circles outline figures in detailed relief of the nine sporting activities involved. All the figures are superb. This firm also produced a more popular version showing Montreal in the centre medallion with the torch-bearer against a garland and an encircling border depicting the competitors competing in various events.

Horseracing has inspired the production of several handsome plates marking the feats of outstanding horses like Nijinsky and Golden Miller. A very rare plate is *The Colonel*. This was a small, neat horse by the 1815 Derby winner Whisker. As a two-year-old The Colonel won three races, but did not race again before the Derby in which he started as favourite at 7–2 with Cadland second favourite at 4–1. There were fifteen runners, with both these horses coming to the post as if locked together. The judge pronounced a dead-heat with a run-off later that afternoon. The Colonel again started favourite at 6–5 on, but in the last fifty yards Cadland came through to win by a neck. The Colonel started favourite for the St Leger which he won. In 1829 he was bought by King George IV to run in the Ascot Cup only to be beaten by Zinganee. A few years later he was exported to Germany. The commemorative plate shows the horse and jockey Bill Scott with the long stirrups of that time. The wording across the top half reads, 'His Majesty's Horse Colonel'.

Another very rare plate is *Faugh-a-Ballagh*. This horse failed to run in the 1844 Derby won by Orlando after a flurry of fraud and intrigue,

(*opposite*): The Olympic Games invariably inspire a wide range of commemorative items. The XXI Olympiad at Montreal was no exception. This plate, simple in design, depicts round the rim the Gold Medal sports.

MONTREAL
OLYMPIAD XXI

but made amends by winning the St Leger, a feat that was commemorated by the plate showing the horse.

The Grand National is featured on a plate produced by Aynsley in support of the Grand National Aintree Campaign. It is encircled by reproductions of original paintings by Margaret Barrett showing horses negotiating the formidable Aintree jumps, the theme being inspired by Michael Gillow's poem which is set out in the centre medallion:

As Regiments of Horse have charged
the gates of Hell, so heroes long gone
hence from here have battled just as well.
Across the Melling Road they go, full gallop in a line
to take the mighty fences that chill us to the spine.
At Bechers Brook they lengthen stride to try and meet it right
for those in front who galloped on have disappeared from sight.
The Turn is now upon them, they'll swing their horse in line
for across the turf at Aintree lies the famous Valentine.
The open ditch gives none to spare, the next will take its toll
and then there is the famous Chair where horse and jockeys roll.
Four miles and more they have to go with stamina and pace
but only one will write his name
and win this famous race.

More sedate is the Penny Farthing 100 Years Commemorative Plate that was commissioned by *The Antique Dealer and Collector's Guide* and produced by Mason's Ironstone China Company in February 1972 with a limited edition of 1000. The outer rim has seven illustrations of this ungainly machine with the centre medallion showing two men competing in a closely contested race. The dates 1872–1972 appear at the top of the plate and lower down there is a lower caption: One Hundred Years of the Penny Farthing's.

Coalport produced a striking commemorative plate marking the 150th Anniversary of the Oxford and Cambridge Boat Race with a

(*opposite*): Grand National Plate from original paintings by Margaret Barrett.

1872   1972
ONE HUNDRED YEARS
OF THE PENNYFARTHING

limited edition of 2500 pieces. Like the Century of Centuries cricketing plates, detailed results of each year are shown on the blades that encircle the centre medallion depicting the start of the Boat Race as a gun is fired, with spectators of the last century in a frenzy of excitement. Being somewhat biased I am tempted to say that the Dark Blues appear to have jumped the gun, but doubtless justice will take its course by Hammersmith Bridge.

There are other commemorative plates to be found whilst firms like Coalport and Royal Worcester produce fresh themes from time to time. The depiction of events and personalities so often forgotten has an overall effect of considerable historic appeal.

(*opposite*): This Penny Farthing 100-years Commemorative Plate was designed in imaginative fashion by S. Davies for a limited edition of 1000.

CHAPTER 6

LAWN TENNIS

Would-be collectors of lawn tennis memorabilia might be well advised to visit the Lawn Tennis Museum at the All-England Club in Wimbledon if only to see what lines to follow, though sadly some of the items rarely come on the market. A good starting-point is to recall how it all began. Millions of television viewers watch the Wimbledon fortnight, yet not many can link the action with the events of the morning of 24 July 1868. Whitmore Jones and his cousin, Henry Jones, met in the office of J.W. Walsh, editor of *The Field*, with the idea of forming a croquet club. The suggestion was approved, the only snag being the necessity of a ground within easy distance of London. Walsh offered to help. For a fee of five sovereigns, a member of *The Field* staff would see what was available, whilst he would establish the legal constitution of such a club and consult the MCC on the subject.

A month later the progress report was hardly encouraging. Approaches had been made to Crystal Palace, Prince's Club in Hans Place, and the Royal Toxophilite in Regent's Park. The response had been negative. The only firm offer was six acres in Holland Park at a rent of £500 a year. It was too expensive. The search continued after another payment of five sovereigns. Almost a year later an option was obtained on four acres of land at Wimbledon at a rent of £50 a year rising to £100. The offer was accepted. The committee guaranteed £600 and a further £425 for laying-out the ground. The club was named the All-England Croquet Club. In 1875 Henry Jones proposed that a portion of the ground be set aside for lawn tennis and badminton. £25 was allocated for equipment. The same Mr Jones urged that a bathroom was

(*opposite*): A very ordinary jug that nevertheless reflects styles and fashions of days when tennis was just a game to be enjoyed.

essential. He offered to adapt a shed, previously used for *The Field* gun-trials, and be responsible for all the expense involved in return for the bath fees during the year, presumably keeping a record of the number of bathers.

In 1877 the name was changed to All-England Croquet and Lawn Tennis Club with committee membership limited to lawn tennis members, and the Rules of Lawn Tennis formulated by the MCC were adopted. Later that year *The Field* editor proposed that a Lawn Tennis Championship be held. Henry Jones was nominated as referee. Walsh arranged for a Challenge Cup to be donated and a special code of rules was drawn-up, differing from the MCC version and persisting in essence for over a century. The Championship was scheduled from Monday, 9 July to Thursday 12 July, play being suspended on the Friday and Saturday as it clashed with the Eton and Harrow cricket match at Lord's. The final was postponed until 19 July when Spencer Gore became the first champion by beating W.C. Marshall. Unlike the Wimbledon champions of today who receive some £70,000 and are still dissatisfied, Gore contended himself with the trophy – the Gold Champion Plate valued at twelve guineas – and the honour of winning.

All these people are dead and gone, but the memorabilia of their times make the foundation of any collection. The champions and players of the past possess a unique appeal. To know something of these figures adds significance to any find associated with them. During the Wimbledon championships comparisons are often made. For all-round excellence I would put the clock back and question whether Bill Tilden has ever been equalled. For ten years he never knew defeat in a championship or Davis Cup match. He had the build of a champion, huge in stature, with the agility of a much lighter man. His drawing-power was extraordinary, rather like Jack Nicklaus in golf, whilst the impact of his personality affected opponents before a ball was struck. Elsworth Vines was one of the hardest strikers of a tennis ball, and had mastered the art of the unbroken rhythmic swing. His timing reflected superb mind and muscle co-ordination. Fred Perry was outstanding, but his game lacked the finished completeness of Tilden and Vines. He fell short of inspired greatness. His game was technically, almost mechanically correct, but lacked the fury of the natural genius. René Lacoste was indefatigable. If history had to remember the Frenchman by one stroke, the choice would be the back-hand. It embodied the essence of stroke-exe-

(*left*): Rene Lacoste completed the Four Musketeers of 'Toto' Brugnon, Jean Borotra and Henri Cochet and stormed the Centre Court. (*right*): 1920 saw the first challenge of that tennis giant, Big Bill Tilden, the supreme champion.

cution. Lacoste studied his opponents with the thoroughness of a boxer piercing a guard with scientific accuracy. Few men on the Centre Court have shown such calm confidence. He was a master technician.

Henri Cochet was different. His game was as enigmatic as his personality. Reflecting the insouciance peculiar to France, Cochet was the opportunist of the courts, bringing off the miracle shot then equally capable of playing a stroke that would make a parks player blush. Donald Budge was prominent in the years immediately preceding the Second World War, but his domination did not coincide with a vintage period. Greatness in 1938 did not equal the standards of 1930. Bunny

Austin was one of those affected. His service was possibly the most laboured seen on the Centre Court.

As for the women, Suzanne Lenglen in her day loomed above all others of her sex, like the domination of Martina Navratilova. The French player was the embodiment of graceful perfection. Helen Wills Moody recaptured something of Lenglen's impersonal greatness, but her game was on a lower plane. The same can be said of Helen Jacobs, though her strokes had a more pugnacious stamp. Kay Menzies likewise touched the hem in a more feminine way. In contrast Alice Marble personified masculine vigour in shot-making, a trait continued by players like Pauline Betz, Margaret du Pont, Louise Brough and Doris Hart. The freshness of Maureen Connolly introduced the incisive approach of the naturalness of youth. Later thumbnail impressions recall the flashing Latin elegance of Maria Bueno, the tireless persistence of Margaret Court with her four Grand Slam Championships in 1970, the sheer delight of that moment of victory when Virginia Wade reaped the reward for years of endeavour. Today the courts are dominated by such players as John McEnroe, Chris Evert Lloyd, Jimmy Connors, Ivan Lendl, Tracy Austin, Pam Shriver, Jo Durie, and the veteran, Billie Jean King.

The essence of any collection is to accumulate visual reminders of the past. In the case of the players, enough photographs in postcard form are in existence to build up a fascinating gallery. Every year at the Wimbledon championships photographs of the current champions are available. It thus becomes a matter of working backwards, gradually filling in the gaps with· early champions a bonus. Rarities would be players like William and Ernest Renshaw who dominated the courts in the 1880s and influenced tactical strategies in the game: the Australian genius Norman E. Brookes, and Maurice McLoughlin known as the 'Californian Comet' who won the American championship in 1911–1913. Equally significant was the influence of the Docherty brothers in the 1890s. Among the lady players Lottie Dod was champion in 1887/ 91/93; Mrs Lambert Chambers was seven times champion; others must include Maud Watson – 1884/85, and Blanche Bingly – 1886/89/94/ 97/99. There is no shortage of names, only supply.

Tennis prints can be attractive, like the one showing the final of the 1884 Wimbledon Singles between H.F. Lawford and Willie Renshaw. There was no mistaking Lawford with his trousers tucked into his stockings and his cap resembling a pith helmet. Immensely strong, he was

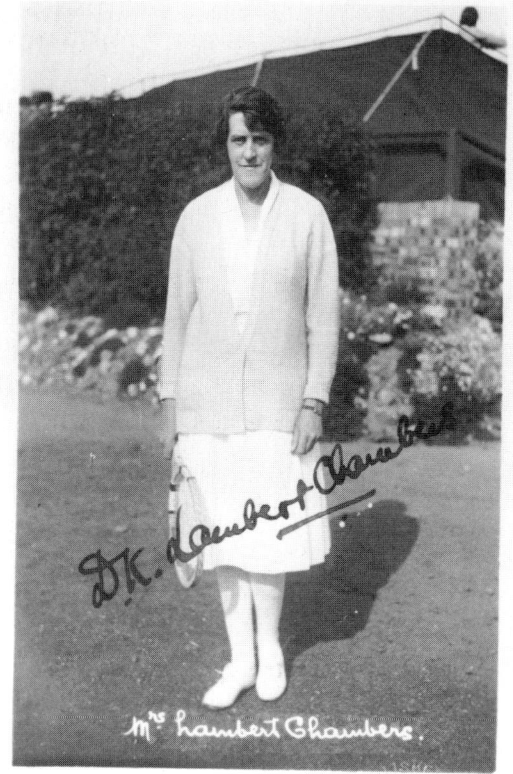

(*left*): Dorothy Round remembered by her Wimbledon Singles win in 1934 against Helen Jacobs. Fred Perry also won the Men's Singles. (*right*): Mrs Lambert Chambers, three times Wimbledon champion as Dolly Douglas and four times after her marriage.

noted for his vicious forehand drive, only on this occasion he lost to Renshaw 6–0, 6–4, 9–7.

George du Maurier executed a charming pen drawing *Le Coeuer Léger*, showing two young tennis players chatting. More exacting was the watercolour of Prince George and Princess Augusta of Cambridge by G. Tielmann showing the children playing with rackets. Alexander M. Rossi painted a watercolour of a pretty young girl with auburn hair with a racket held in somewhat untennis-like fashion, but the style is typical of the 1880s.

Ceramic figures on the whole are somewhat fussy and over-winsome, many of continental origin, though a pair in the art deco style of 1920 shows a man with outstretched racket trying to retrieve a strong shot from his lady opponent. Most of it is garden party stuff but nevertheless should be included.

Items of equipment can be interesting including square-headed and fish-handle rackets, and an all-metal racket with metal strings, nut and spring tensioner, and with a canvas-covered handle. Reaction today to such a weapon would be on a par with the public outcry at Dennis Lillee's aluminium cricket bat in Australia. Occasionally it is possible to come across the programme for the first Wimbledon championship meeting in 1877, also the lawn tennis championships souvenir of 1914 in which the advertisements are more interesting than the text and illustrations. A modern but attractive Bilston and Battersea enamel box commemorating the first lawn tennis championship of 1877 has a frieze of players round the base showing the contestants in the garb of that day; on the cover is a reproduction of what is meant to be the finalists though in fact the original print was the 1884 final between Renshaw and Lawford. Inside the cover is engraved the result: Spencer C. Gore beat W. C. Marshall in the first Men's Singles 6–1, 6–2, 6–4, with presumably an action study of the winner on the inside base. Altogether it is a collector's piece, like the late nineteenth-century plaques showing the players in detail.

Literature of the game is fairly plentiful, but mostly dull and factual, failing to do justice to the grace and fluency of the sport. It needs the pen of Bernard Darwin or Neville Cardus to introduce some literary style.

CHAPTER 7

THE LEGEND OF W. G. GRACE

It is difficult to convey to others the personality of an individual, to know what feature to isolate. For instance, we seldom realise how vital yet how incommunicable an element is the quality of voice. It is regrettable that those who knew the outstanding figures of the past ignored the fact that almost a third part of the character of any individual is bound up with the tone or inflection of his or her speaking voice. Even Boswell, who sketched a vivid physical pen-portrait of his companion, did not enlarge on the sound-picture of Dr Johnson thundering, wheezing and panting. We know that Napoleon spoke in a low voice, the Corsican accent only asserting itself when roused by anger. We know that Shelley's voice was shrill and Byron's soft. The resonant tones of Tennyson's voice were blended with the broad vowels of the Lincolnshire wolds, whilst Bismarck could only summon the accents of a child. These fragmentary allusions underline the value for posterity of the recorded voices of men like Churchill, Gandhi, Stalin, Hitler, and Smuts.

In the realm of sport, when the time comes to live in the season of reverie, I shall remember Bernard Darwin, not by his stooping figure or distinctive head, but by the cadence of a voice in which was mingled the grace of the scholar and the discrimination of a man of taste. I single out Darwin in this context because not long before he died I asked him what W.G. Grace was like away from the world of cricket. The condensed vignette recalled the high-piping notes of W.G.'s voice, an unexpected contrast to the frame of a man who physically dominated the Victorian scene. Darwin recalled eyes fierce and accusatory with their fire mitigated by deep lines of character encircled, if not embedded, by an aggressive beard. The impressive length of head from chin to crown was accentuated by the beard which a backward carriage of his head on broad shoulders projected forwards, whilst the beetling eye-brows, prominent nose and hunched shoulders gave him a hawk-like look.

W.G. Grace was one of the most remarkable of English cricketers. Gloucestershire-born at Downend, a small village near Bristol, his father was a country doctor and keen cricketer. In 1847, a year before W.G. was on the scene, he amalgamated the local club with the West Gloucestershire County Club, then founded in 1862 the original Gloucestershire County Club for which W.G. made his first appearance at the age of fourteen. The unrestrained originality of Grace's approach to the game was unmistakable. His stance at the wicket was individualistic with left boot edged up from the heel and right boot pointing in the direction of cover point, which he argued made it easier to swing to leg.

No one could say that Grace was universally popular. He could be controversial, cantankerous and stubborn, but invariably a rugged charm came through in the end. A tactical opportunist and captain of rare achievement, he is regarded as the greatest English cricketer, a claim that can neither be substantiated nor refuted, but the title is irrelevant. Statistics speak for themselves. Any batsman who can score centuries for thirty-eight years is in a class of his own, to say nothing of scoring a thousand runs in a month at the age of forty-nine. His innings were made against top-class bowling, including the full force of Spofforth who, if history does not lie, made the likes of Truman and Lillie look

Interesting study of W.G. Grace as a bearded young man.

medium-paced. Rounding off the figures, Grace scored 126 centuries in first-class cricket: 54,896 runs averaging 39·55 an innings; 2,876 wickets at 17·92 runs apiece; highest scores were 344, 318 not out, 301, and carried his bat 17 times through a completed innings. In Tests against Australia, he averaged 32·39 including two centuries. His last match was between Eltham and Grove Park on 25 July 1914. On a fiery wicket, he scored, according to Wisden, '69 not out in a total of 155 for six wickets'.

The fact that these figures have been beaten more than once does not affect his role in English cricket. W.G. was cricket. His name was known across the length and breadth of the country, and this at a time when the public was not spoon-fed by newspapers, radio and television. Players did not rely on public relations officers. There was no Victorian equivalent to Kerry Packer or Mark MacCormick. Controversial interviews did not appear in Sunday newspapers. Without publicity aids, Grace was a national institution as noticeable as the Albert Memorial. It was an England of peaceful country content, of the carriage-and-pair, of the rule of the squire. It was an age of individuality as mirrored in the *Vanity Fair* cartoons. In many ways it is odd that the Diamond Jubilee of 1897 did not bring a knighthood as fitting reward for the man who made cricket England's national game. Maybe it was because in certain circles, sport as such was confined to self-contained areas. The name of Grace was popularly acclaimed, but once the flannels were off, he faded into anonymity. His contemporaries included such men as Tennyson, Morris, Millais, Browning, Hardy, Meredith, Leighton, Coventry Patmore, Burne-Jones, Stevens and Rossetti, a parallel XI of rare talents, but their paths did not cross. Grace was a Matthew Arnold philistine. The label did not bother the Old Man. He was content with his national identity, a mighty Victorian in his own right. In one sense all eminent Victorians made strong impressions. There was Tennyson's cloak and sombrero. Gladstone's collar, Matthew Arnold's whiskers, Disraeli's forelock, and Newman's ascetic frailty. The bust of Grace in the Memorial Gallery at Lord's gives a glimpse of the personality behind a caliph's beard, but fails to convey the gargantuan girth that dwarfed his contemporaries.

In every way W.G. Grace is an ideal subject on which to make a specialised collection of cricket ephemera. There are still many items to be found that fill in the background of this legend. Giants like Alfred

Mynn and Fuller Pilch loom dimly, but they left little tangible for later generations. W.G. was the link between these two cricketing eras. As a child he recalled the arrival of Clarke's All-England Eleven in Bristol to play against a local twenty-two led by Dr Grace. The recollection of men playing in tall hats was confirmed by his mother's scrap-books which show top-hatted George Parr, Caffyn, Willsher, Clarke, Box and Julius Caesar. She was also given a book inscribed 'Presented to Mrs. Grace by William Clarke, Secretary, All-England Eleven'. In a real sense Grace's parents laid a *golfing* foundation. After his death Sir Stanley Jackson aptly phrased the inscription on the Memorial Gate at Lord's:

To the Memory of
William Gilbert Grace
The Great Cricketer

Chronology

1848	Born at Downend
1854	Saw All-England Eleven
1863	Played against All-England Eleven
1864	First Match in London
1865	Played for Gentlemen and England
1869	Elected to MCC
1871	Outstanding Year
1872	Visit to Canada and United States of America
1873	Married his cousin, Agnes Day. First visit to Australia
1876	839 runs in three innings
1879	Began practice as doctor
1880	First Test Match. Death of Fred Grace
1891	Second visit to Australia
1895	1,000 runs in May. Hundredth 100 & National Testimonial
1899	Jubilee Match
1899	Last Test Match. Last Match for Gloucestershire and inauguration of London County
1905	End of London County
1906	Last Match for Gentlemen v Players
1914	Last innings at Eltham
1915	Death at Nottingham

Typically posed study of W.G. Grace in the Beldam mould. Considering his girth, W.G. was remarkably agile.

Auction sales in London of Cricketana usually offer several lots linked with Grace, some repetitive, others rare. Occasionally a relic is found in an antique shop, whilst local sales in country houses can produce surprises. The following examples give an indication of what has come on the market. The commemorative plate *Century of Centuries* with a blue and white transfer band of cricket bats, stumps, bails and cricket balls with the centuries listed and a central portrait of Grace is a rarity – 23 cm in diameter, it usually fetches between £550 and £650. A similar pattern is used on a small cotton tablecloth. A head and shoulders likeness of Grace is in the centre encircled by a hundred cricket bats giving the date and place when the centuries were scored, plus a somewhat flowery tribute. The price varies but it has been bought at just under £1,000. Occasionally the hammer has fallen at roughly half that figure.

An interesting item was the detailed menu of a banquet held on 24 June 1895 at the Victoria Rooms, Clifton to celebrate the 'One Hundredth Century' by Grace against Somerset on 17 May 1895, with the Duke of Beaufort presiding. The toasts were numerous – 'The Queen', 'The Prince and Princess of Wales', 'The Bishop and Ministers of Religion', 'English Sport', preceded 'Mr W.G. Grace', proposed by the Duke. The food was plentiful, the wine list adequate, all the centuries were listed, the words of a W.G. ballad printed, and a typical photograph of the Old Man completed the package.

The range of Grace relics is extensive. A colourful biscuit figure, probably Austrian, shows him standing in pads with MCC cap, unmistakable beard, and bat raised. It measures 23·4 cm, date about 1900. An unusual item seen several times in London auction rooms is a cast-iron pub table with a circular wooden top – not an object of beauty, but of interest to a collector because of portraits of Grace moulded on the three legs, initialled 'W.G.'. It measures 76 cm in diameter, date about 1880. Not to be outdone, a nineteenth-century pub sign 'The Cricketer' 128 cm has also been on the market. The central panel shows a cricket match with Grace at the wicket. The bidding was brisk, the final price of £170 being almost double the estimated figure.

Another collector's piece is a handsome late Victorian Doulton jug,

(*opposite*): Cover of the Banquet menu that offered a formidable number of courses, toasts, speeches and ballads.

G.C.C.
BANQUET
HELD ON
MONDAY, JUNE 24TH, 1895, at the VICTORIA ROOMS, CLIFTON,
TO
MR. W. G. GRACE
in Celebration of his
ONE HUNDREDTH "CENTURY,"
Completed on GLOUCESTERSHIRE COUNTY GROUND in match
SOMERSETSHIRE v GLOUCESTERSHIRE,
on FRIDAY MAY 17TH 1895.
HIS GRACE THE DUKE OF BEAUFORT, K.G.,
President

sepia in colour with dark brown rim, decorated with oval portraits of George Griffin, K.S. Ranjitsinhji and W.G. Grace, foilage, and impressed mark Doulton, Lambeth, England 1891. It measures 18 cm. Apart from the excellent likeness of Grace, it is interesting to see George Giffen. Born in 1859, he was one of Australia's major all-rounders. In thirty-one Tests against England he claimed 103 wickets for 27 runs apiece, and a batting average of 23. In 1893 he anticipated leg-theory tactics by bowling off-breaks round the wicket to four short legs. He was the first Australian to take 10 wickets in an innings.

From time to time a Staffordshire-type figure of Grace appears in the sale-rooms. It is of poor quality, indifferently modelled and only identifiable by the beard. Better value are the numerous commemorative pottery mugs, even the modern reproductions sold in the shop at Lord's. Occasionally one of W.G.'s bats is offered. Some are suspect, though not the *Shaw and Shrewsbury* bat that Grace wielded to make 159 not out for Lord Sheffield's team against Victoria at Melbourne on 27–28 November 1891, now suitably inscribed on the reverse. A fine collector's item is the small bronze statue of Grace specially commissioned by Cricket Fine Art from James Butler, RA in a limited edition of 250, though I question whether Grace would have been flattered by the likeness. More personal is a vulcanite pipe with the stem shaped as a cricket bat, inscribed 'W.G.G. Aet 47 AD, 1895'. The bowl is moulded in the form of Grace's head. Ashtrays are numerous. The Lord's shop has a modern version showing Grace in traditional stance with left toe cocked. Kepple of Bristol produced a heavy spherical pottery type, again with the bat half raised, and autographed at the base.

Another addition to a Grace collection comes from Bilston, the South Staffordshire centre of the enamelling trade where choice snuff-boxes and similar items of japanned metal with enamel decoration on the lids have been produced for centuries. The cricketing box is a modern replica of this art. Inside the hinged lid in flowing cursive hand is the captain, 'A Village Cricket Match at the turn of the 19th Century'. Outlined at the base of the circular box is the likeness of a cricketer either bowling with an exaggerated low action or a fieldsman hurling the ball at the wicket. Crossed bats and balls decorate the green sides. The cover shows

(*opposite*): Contemporary pottery interpretation of the game. In spite of his technique, the batsman sports an M.C.C. cap.

a village match with the batsman resembling Grace executing a stroke that did little for his reputation.

In 1873 a committee drawn from each first-class cricketing county established the residency rules on county cricket, the representative for Gloucestershire being W.G. Grace. The commemoration of the hundredth anniversary of this event was marked by the issue of several collectable items. To honour county cricket 1873–1973, the Post Office featured Dr Grace on three special stamps, the drawing on each stamp being taken from a series of one hundred sketches – *A Century of Grace* – by Harry Furniss. The first day of issue of the stamps was 16 May 1973 with the cancellation carried out by the Post Office at Lord's Cricket Ground.

Letters and autographs frequently come on the market. A postcard written and signed by Grace and postmarked Sydenham, 26 March 1899 was sold for £45. A signed letter, dated 1 December of the same year and addressed to H.A. Budden, fetched £60. Another written and signed postcard, dated 31 October 1899, headed London County Cricket Club, and addressed to the same individual realised £48. A signed card was knocked down for £45. A letter and envelope, both bordered with black, dated 16 July, 1900, written to Andrew Weston, sympathising with his illness, but declining an invitation, was sold for £60. Another epistle, dated 1893 and addressed to A.J. Lancaster, secretary of Kent, dealing with fixture arrangements, raised £40. A letter dated August 1896 which argued the case for Davis playing in a match on the County Ground found a purchaser for £55. A framed telegram from Grace to his wife informing her of his score of 140 not out for the United South on 17 July 1894 found its way into someone's collection for £45. Such personal fragments of Grace's everyday life are continually being unearthed and have a collector's value of between £50 and £60 apiece.

Old photographs are particularly rewarding, not only for showing W.G. in action but capturing something of the nineteenth-century atmosphere of the game, the spectators and the grounds – not a romantic idea of what it might have been like, but the real thing. *Vanity Fair* published a caricature of Grace in the issue of 9 June 1877. It is by 'Spy', or Sir Leslie Ward, and reflects his early style that concentrated

(*opposite*): Correspondence in Grace's bold handwriting are fairly common, often under London County Cricket Club heading.

LONDON COUNTY CRICKET CLUB.

" St. Andrews,"
Lawrie Park Road,
Sydenham, March 25th 1905

We have so many pictures, that
I really cannot undertake any more.
Very glad to hear you have a good
ground etc. With kind regards,
I am
                    Yours truly
                    W. G. Grace

London County Cricket Club.

"St. Andrew's," Lawrie Park Road,
SYDENHAM, Oct 31th   1899

Dear Budden
            I have not heard a word
re Bedford match since I saw you
In haste
                    Yours truly
                    W. G. Grace

This very fine plate, blue-printed and lavishly gilded, commemorating the Century of Centuries, was issued in 1895 by the Coalport Porcelain Works.

on the element of caricature. His later studies were like orthodox portraits, more accurate in detail but lacking character. The colour lithograph is worthy of any Grace collection, likewise a print of the well-known painting by Archibald Stuart-Wortley, commissioned by the Committee of MCC in 1888, exhibited in the Royal Academy in 1890 and part of the Sir Jeremiah Colman Collection of cricket paintings presented by his son to the Imperial Cricket Memorial Gallery at Lord's. It shows Grace at the crease in his traditional stance, the giant who came on the scene a year after over-arm bowling was officially accepted.

Of the making of books about W.G. Grace there is no end, but the very quantity is an encouragement to anyone attempting to make a specialised collection. The following list could be an aid.

The Memorial Biography of Dr. W.G. Grace, edited by Lord Hawke, Lord Harris and Sir Home Gordon. Constable 1919.

Cricket by W.G. Grace. Arrowsmith 1891.

A Few Short Runs by Lord Harris. Murray 1921.

W.G. Grace. A biography by W. Methven Brownlee. Iliffe 1887.

Life Worth Living by C.B. Fry. Eyre & Spottiswoode 1939.

The History of a Hundred Centuries by W.G. Grace. Upcott Gill 1895.

W.G. Grace by Bernard Darwin. Duckworth 1934.

Kings of Cricket by Richard Daft. Arrowsmith 1893.

Cricket by Neville Cardus. Longsmans Green 1930.

'W.G.' Cricketing Reminiscences and Personal Recollections by W.G. Grace. James Bowden 1899.

W.G.'s Little Book by W.G. Grace. George Newnes 1907

Dr. W.G. Grace by Acton Wye (Bijou Biographies), Henry J. Drane 1901.

W.G. Grace by Clifford Bax. Phoenix House 1952.

A History of Cricket by H.S. Althan and E.W. Swanton. George Allen & Unwin 1926.

The Jubilee Book of Cricket by K.S. Ranjitsinhji. Wm Blackwood and Sons 1897.

Talks with Old English Cricketers by A.W. Pullin (Old Ebor), Blackwood 1900.

The Graces, E.M., W.G., and G.F. by A.G. Powell and S. Canynge Caple. The Cricket Book Society 1948.

Cricket: A Popular Handbook of the Game by W.G. Grace and others. Religious Tract Society 1881.

The Game of Cricket, with Introduction by Sir Norman Birkett. Batsford 1955.

A History of the Gloucestershire County Cricket Club, 1870–1949, by S. Canynge Caple. Littlebury, Worcester 1949.

Long Innings by Sir Pelham Warner. Harrap 1951.

Lord's 1787–1945 by Sir Pelham Warner. Harrap 1946.

The Book of Cricket: A Gallery of Great Players by Denzil Batchelor. Collins 1952.

Gentlemen v. Players 1806–1949 by Sir Pelham Warner. Harrap 1950.

Concerning Cricket by John Arlott. Longmans Green 1949.

On and off the Field by Sir Henry Leveson-Gower. Stanley Paul 1953.

The Complete Cricketer by Albert E. Knight. Methuen 1906.

History of Mangotsfield and Downend by Rev. A. Emlyn Jones. W.S. Mack & Co, Bristol 1899.

With Bat and Ball by George Giffen. Ward, Lock & Co. 1898.

Cricket in Ireland by Patrick Hone. Kerryman Press 1955.

Talking of Cricket by Ian Peebles. Museum Press 1953.

Pebbles on the Shore by Alpha of the Plough (A.G. Gardiner), Dent 1917.

They Made Cricket by G.D. Martineau. Museum Press 1956.

Victorian England: Portrait of an Age by G.M. Young. Oxford University Press 1936.

This selection of books reflects not only the role played by W.G. Grace, but gives a cross-section of the traditions, ritual and subtlety of this connoisseur's game.

One last rarity for the Grace collector. The Stevengraph silk shows him standing at the wicket on the occasion of his century of centuries in 1895. The full title Dr W.G. Grace was first listed on label 31–29 of 1896. Although it must have been popular and therefore relatively common, it is rare to find it on offer today. At auction the silk fetches three figures, but tucked away in old junk shops there must be many going for a song – which is part of the appeal of collecting.

CHAPTER 8

STIRRUP CUPS

Stirrup cups offer plenty of scope to the potential collector, but background knowledge is essential. Even an inkling of their past history helps enormously in the search for the many variations of drinking cups that can be found. Their hey-day was the reign of George IV when everyone from the monarch to the humble peasant was interested in sporting activities; every phase of blood-sport from fox-hunting to wagers on cock-fighting. It was a rumbustious period of hard drinking after the chase; punch – spiced to taste, wine, and strong ale in drinking cups modelled after the heads of various creatures linked with their sport by silversmiths.

The earliest of these stirrup-cups date from the mid-eighteenth century, choice pieces made by hand from individual plates of silver. The style was elegant with the finishing-touch of a rimmed collar to carry personal inscription of a special occasion. The idea was adopted by each Hunt and periodically it is possible to find handsome examples of these models, often bearing a family crest on the head. At the outset fox-masks were the favourites. Coursing became very popular and therefore so did greyhound heads, again bearing identifying inscriptions on the collars.

About 1775 these silver stirrup-cups were copied in soft porcelain at Derby and Chelsea. Sizes varied from three inches to a foot in length, coloured in tawny red with gold-banded rim. In a Chelsea sale of 1782 the catalogue listed 'One pair of foxes heads for drinking cups, small, 6s'. A larger size was quoted at 8s 6d a pair. Bone china examples date from the early nineteenth century, recognisable by the white translucent finish. Derby produced naturalistic fox-heads, often with pink collars and yellow eyes, glazed in pearly white. Other models included plain browns and yellows, glazed inside and with a matt finish. At times

Sporting Stirrup-cups can represent a range of sports. Hound heads were favourites with fox heads during the early 19th century.

it is difficult to attribute a trade mark or name. The Derby crown and crossed batons are unmistakable, likewise the Rockingham griffin in puce marks. These are usually on realistically coloured heads incisively modelled. Some are lavender glazed.

Staffordshire potters widened the range of interest. Their fox-head drinking cups were decorated with natural colours, grey or black muzzles and pink ears. As many as thirty Staffordshire potters were involved, but it is difficult to identify individual styles. One head somewhat crudely modelled with green glaze markings has been attributed to Thomas Whieldon, but the claim is questionable. It is safe to say that those in black basalt are by Josiah Wedgwood; those with a bright black glaze come from J. & J. Jackson of Burslem about 1790; larger heads with reddish and black markings are usually Lambeth and Fulham. The fox-heads have a variety of collars. The most common colours are yellow, black, blue and white, occasionally gilt, whilst pink lustre was popular at the beginning of the nineteenth century. Those who could not afford sterling silver or Sheffield plate could buy silver lustre cups after 1820. Most had hand-impressed marking round the rim. A few years later dark brown pottery cups of copper lustre and dappled silver were produced.

Fox-heads gave way to the creatures of other sports. Hound-heads in naturalistic colours were very popular. They were produced by Rockingham, Derby, Coalport and several Staffordshire potters. The last named made hound-heads in black and grey with reddish-brown the most common. One series had black ears and a light muzzle. Collars were yellow, red and black, occasionally gilded and with the name of the hound inscribed. A Derby hound-head had a pierced gold collar for mounting a silver name-plate.

Greyhound stirrup-cups are attractive in grey or yellow grey with light-brown collars often inscribed with the owner's name. Copeland & Garrett produced some striking models with particularly long necks about 1835. Derby made large bull-terrier heads in bone china. Setters' heads were others' choice, Rockingham making one in natural colours

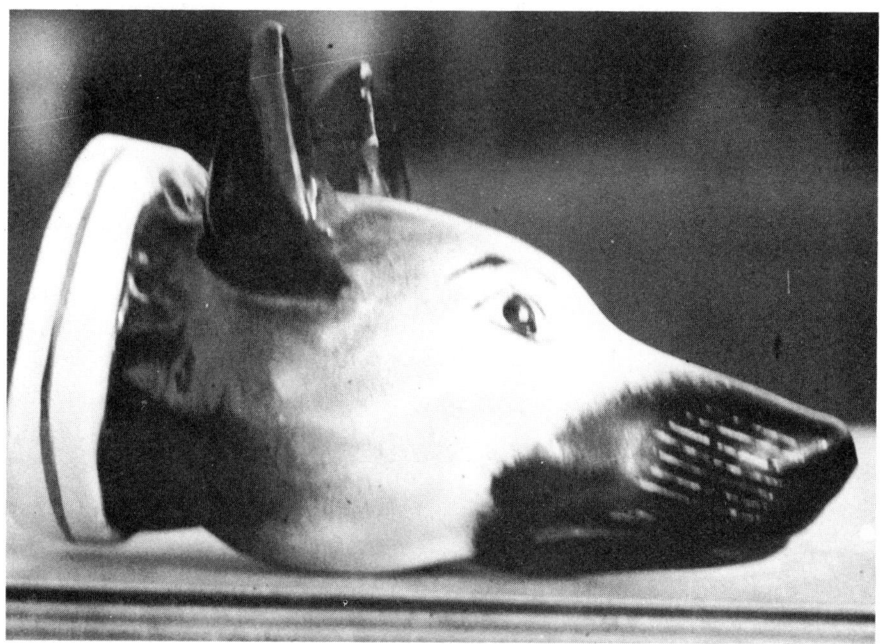

Lifelike fox heads often hard earthenware enamelled in naturalistic reddish brown. Collars partly gilded or enamelled in plain colours.

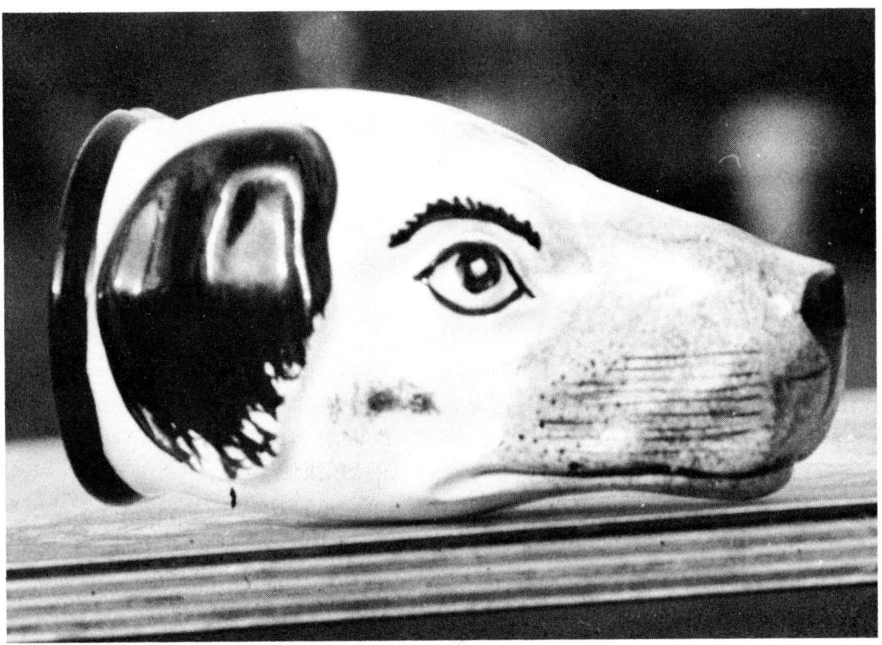

Hound heads are painted naturalistically with collars often recording in gold letters the names of popular hounds.

with the griffin mark in red. The country squire might fancy the Dalmatian cup. Bull-baiting devotees were offered a bulldog head glazed in brown with yellow collar and eyes. The Rockingham version is realistically modelled in bone china, whilst Staffordshire potters had white bulldog heads in varying sizes.

The hare-head drinking cup was introduced by Ralph Wood II. It was not particularly impressive with indifferent modelling, fawn-grey glaze, and close-set ears. The earthenware model at the beginning of the nineteenth century had a large loop handle flanked by the ears enamelled in several shades of brown. A later version had upright ears which served as a handle. Derby produced the loop-handled model in porcelain in the 1770s, enamelled in fawn and russet shades with the cup-mouth touched with gold. They followed with bone china pieces, the naturalistic colours having the crown and cross batons mark, with D in red; date after 1815. The Georgian deer-stalker had stirrup-cups portraying deer or stag-heads without horns. Whieldon produced some poor earthenware models in cream and manganese, usually with very small ears. E. Mayer of Hanley (1770–1813) introduced a series of fawn-coloured heads with decorative collars of wine motifs. Silver-lustre was also popular, again with decorative rims.

Anglers were remembered with trout-head cups. The finest are Derby in naturalistic colours with pink fins and spotted back and gilt-rimmed band sometimes inscribed 'The Angler's Delight'. Staffordshire potters produced white bone glazed china models with speckled mouth and gilt fins. Fulham had a brown glazed stoneware version.

The boxing supporter was identified with a cup shaped as a clenched fist. Leeds introduced a number of horses' heads, whilst cock-fighting enthusiasts had a cock's head, and bull-baiting a choice of brown or black glazed earthenware bears' heads.

There is a wide enough selection of sporting stirrup-cups to make an unusual representative collection.

MOLINEUX

TOM CRIBB

CHAPTER 9

THE LURE OF THE PRIZE-RING

The collector of pugilistic pottery has a choice of subjects in a variety of different ceramic forms made by enterprising potters who anticipated a ready market for figures of popular pugilists, together with jugs and tankards commemorating the more important fights. The fact that each piece can be accurately dated adds greatly to the interest. Bare-knuckle fighting by today's standards was a brutal institution, but is nevertheless part of the evolution of the sport. In that sense the old prize-ring was a genuine expression of English life.

Contemporary prints represent another rich field. Boxing attracted scores of aquatints like the rare *The Interior of the Fives Court*. This was the recognised centre for prize-ring devotees. Young boxers often were matched for their first fight. Benefits were held, producing as much as £200 a night. Those who wished to watch in comfort paid a guinea and can be seen behind windows high up. In the centre of the court a stage was erected four feet from the ground. The chronicler in *Tom Spring's Life in London* informs us that 'The combatants were stripped to the waist, the sports beginning with the third and fourth rate exhibitors, who gratified the spectators with a glove-fight, for which they were rewarded with showers of either copper or silver, and sometimes both, according to their merits, then came the "stars", fighting their battles o'er again, and exhibiting the very perfection of the art.'

The fighters in the print are Jack Randall and Ned Turner, both of whom had known bare-knuckle fighting. Randall, whom George Borrow called 'King of the Light-weights' and the 'Nonpareil', had beaten Turner on Crawley Downs in 1818 after thirty-four gruelling rounds.

(*opposite*): Tom Molineux, American negro prizefighter. Tom Cribb, champion prize-fighter of England from 1808 to 1824. Retired unbeaten and became a London publican.

Many of the foreground figures in the print are portraits of personalities connected with fighting. We learn from a key that Jem Belcher is among them, but the famous pugilist died long before the print was made. Incidentally it was at the Fives Court that Belcher lost an eye when playing racquets with a Mr Stewart in July of 1803. Lifeguardsman Shaw, also a champion boxer and identified as one of the soldiers in uniform, was killed at Waterloo. Such mistakes were accepted, for it was customary to commemorate in prints the figures of celebrities who had been popularly connected with the sport. The painting of the Fives Court is by T. Blake, the print by Charles Turner – who, among other important works, engraved twenty-four plates after J.M.W. Turner's *Liber Studiorum*.

Between the years 1805 and 1815 England had cause for pride with men like Nelson and Wellington. Their triumphs had their counterpart with the heyday of the prize-ring. Among many fighters of renown few could equal Tom Cribb, a Gloucestershire man born at Hanham in 1781, who became champion of England at the age of twenty-eight. He retained the title the following year by beating a former champion, Jem Belcher, whom he had thrashed before. His most famous bouts were against Thomas Molineux, a black American who had been a slave in Virginia. Legally freed, Molineux came to England to make a living with his fists and was befriended by Bill Richmond, a fellow negro who had entered the service of the Duke of Northumberland when he was campaigning in America, paid for his education and set him up as a carpenter, later keeping an inn in the West End of London. Miller handled Molineux astutely. He knew the ropes and the pitfalls. He was the first negro boxer of whom there is any record. Their likenesses were drawn and etched by Richard Dighton, prints that are now rare.

Richmond persuaded Cribb to fight Molineux with the championship belt at stake, for £200-a-side on December 10, 1810, the site being Copthall Common, near East Grinstead in Sussex. Some 5000 spectators ignored the torrential rain and gathered round the muddy ring. John Gulley and Joe Ward acted as Cribb's seconds. Molineux had Bill Richmond and Paddington Jones. The referee was Sir Thomas Apreece. Physically both men were well matched – Cribb stood 5 ft 10½ ins; Molineux slightly shorter. Each weighed 14st 2lb. The wet turf made it difficult to keep a stance and falls were frequent, but by the ninth round betting was 6–4 on the negro. By the eighteenth each had taken such punishment that they could only be identified by colour. The Englishman was in a sorry state. In the nineteenth round Cribb was pinned against the ropes. Molineux seized the top rope on either side of his opponent and leant on his body so that Cribb could neither strike or fall. The seconds protested that the men should be separated, but the umpires ruled that a fighter had to fall before he could be touched by a second. The crowd took command by beating the negro's hands with sticks. The grip was relinquished but Molineux benefited from the breather and felled the exhausted Cribb to the ground. Betting on Molineux was now 4–1. The end should have come in the twenty-third round. Cribb had fallen to the ground when his second ran across the ring and accused Richmond of putting bullets in the negro's hands. This was untrue, but the referee had a check to make certain. The delay was to Cribb's advantage. Under prize-ring rules a round ended when a man was knocked down and 30 seconds had elapsed. Cribb recovered; Molineux suffered reaction. The freezing temperature left him shivering. Weakening, he managed to hang on before collapsing in the fortieth round. Tom Cribb had retained the belt, but Molineux should have been the champion. The referee must have spotted the trick, whilst the crowd was anti-Molineux, though the Stock Exchange after the fight made slight amends by giving him a present of £45. Cribb could not be criticised for at the critical moment he was well-nigh unconscious.

The aftermath of this fight was a letter in *The Times* for Christmas Day, 1810.

To Mr Thomas Cribb   St Martin's Street,
Leicester Square.
Dec. 21st, 1810

Sir – My friends think, that had the weather on last Tuesday, the day upon which I contended with you, had not been so unfavourable, I should have won the battle: I, therefore, challenge you to a second meeting, at any time within two months, for such sum as these gentlemen who place confidence in me may be pleased to arrange.

As it is possible this letter may meet the public

eye, I cannot omit the opportunity of expressing a
confident hope, that the circumstances of my being
a different colour to that of a people amongst whom
I have sought protection will not in any way op-
erate to my prejudice.

I am, sir,
Your most obedient, humble servant,
T. Molineux

Witness, J. Scholfield

The challenge was accepted for a purse of 600 guineas. It took place at
Thistleton Gap in Rutland on 28 September 1811. The result was virtually decided during the training period before the bout. Molineux did
not bother with a build-up programme; in fact just before the fight he
ate a whole chicken and an apple pie, and downed plenty of porter.
Cribb had been handled by Captain Barclay, the first trainer to recognise
the value of road work. He made Cribb walk some twenty miles a day
for a month until he shed 50 pounds from his waistline and took the
scales at 13 stone.

In less than a week after the fight two graphic prints were published.
The progress of the fight is recorded on the second print:

The Close of the Battle or the Champion Triumphant.

1. Round. Sparring for one minute, Crib made play right &
   left, a right handed blow told slightly on the body of Moli-
   neaux, who returned it on the head & a rally followed, the
   Black knocked down by a hit on the throat.

2. Crib shewed first blood from the mouth, a dreadful rally
   Crib put in a good body hit, returned by the Moor on the
   head closeing, Crib thrown.

3. Crib's right eye nearly closed, another rally, the Black def-
   ficent in wind, receives a doubler in the body. Crib damaged
   in both eyes & thrown.

4. Rally, hits exchanged, Crib fell with a slight hit and mani-
   fested first weakness.

5. Ralling renewed Crib fell from a blow & received another in falling.

6. Black fatigued by want of wind, a blow at the body mark doubles him up & is floored by a hit at great length.

7. Black runs in intemperately, receives several violent blows about the neck & Juggler, falls from weakness.

8. Black rallies, Crib nobs him, gets his head under his left arm & fibbed till the Moor fell.

9. Black runs in met with a left handed blow which broke his jaw, and fell like a log.

10. Black with difficulty made an unsuccessful effort & fell from distress.

11. This round ended the fight Black received another knock down, & unable again to stand up.

Such is the eye-witness account of a title-fight that took place in 1811. The ring measured 25 feet square, but the artist allowed imagination a bonus when he showed the seconds and bottle-holders in the ring with the fighters. Sir Thomas Apreece is shown holding a watch. The bout lasted 19 minutes, 10 seconds. Cribb collected £400 for what proved to be his last fight. Captain Barclay netted £10,000. Molineux received £50 from a collection. Three months later Cribb was declared to be 'Champion for Life' at a presentation of a Silver Cup in the Castle Tavern, Holborn. The subsequent career of Molineux was sad. He began to drink heavily and died a few years later in Galway barracks. Tom Cribb became a publican and included among his customers such men as Hazlitt and Byron. He died at his son's house at Woolwich on 11 May 1848. Considering his occupation, sixty-eight was not a bad age.

Apart from prints, these two boxers are commemorated in a number of ways. A striking pair of figures by Enoch Wood show the pugilists stripped to the waist in a slightly crouching attitude with raised fists. A rare figure of Molineux shows him in upright position with blue jerkin buttoned to the neck, yellow breeks, white stockings and black shoes. Another upright action figure of Cribb shows him with fists raised, stripped to the waist, with orange sash and mauve breeks, white stockings and black shoes. Likenesses of both boxers in action appear on transfer-printed cream ware and yellow earthenware jugs. A silver resist lustre jug shows both boxers, with this verse on the reverse side:

Since boxing is a manly game,
and Britons recreation,
By boxing we will raise our fame,
Bove any other nation.
Throw pistols, pomards, swords, a side,
And all such deadly tools;
Let boxing be the Britons pride,
The science of their schools.

Finally a rare portrait of Thomas Cribb was painted on a Chamberlain Worcester plate where Cribb is shown standing stripped to the waist, in a ring on raised ground with a landscape background. The portrait is signed 'H. Chamberlain pinxt' and on the back is inscribed a list of Cribb's victories from 1805 to 1811. The original picture on which the ceramic painting was based was by Douglas Guest. A mezzotint engraved by J. Young was published in 1811.

The print drawn by C. Metz of Thomas Johnson and Isaac Perrins does not exaggerate the comparative size of the two fighters. Their bout at Banbury on 2 October 1789 is regarded as one of the toughest in the history of the prize-ring. Johnson, who came from Derby, was small for a heavyweight champion. He was under 5 ft 9 ins, but weighed more than 14 stone. Perrins, a Birmingham man, scaled some 17 stone and stood 6 ft 2 ins. The fight lasted $1\frac{1}{4}$ hours over sixty-two rounds and was marked by Johnson's uncontrolled temper and doubtful tactics. His attitude was described by Thomas Fewtrell in 1788 as 'fists held before the head, arms nearly extended, legs almost square, body much bent with the breast forward. This has little elegance or manhood in its appearance, and is practised by very few. The body is protected by this more than any other guard; but the head is exposed. Men possessed of uncommon strength in the loins should only accustom themselves to it, as it must fatigue all others.' And so it proved in the case of Perrins. Outclassed, he took terrible punishment; his face 'had scarce the traces left of a human being', but he refused to give in. Eventually his backers and seconds threw in the towel. Johnson's reign as champion lasted from 1785 to 1791, when for six years he was beaten by Ben Brian.

The collector of pugilistic pottery can look for a rare mug with an animated print of this fight, bearing the caption *Johnson & Perrins at Banbury*. It is in the Willett Collection in the Brighton Museum.

A particularly fine bust was made of Ben Caunt. Some $15\frac{1}{2}$ inches high, it too can be seen in the Brighton Museum. This rugged son of a servant of Lord Byron at Newstead looks the bruiser he must have been. Measuring 6 ft 3 ins and weighing 15 stone, he won the Championship of England in 1841 through beating Nick Ward in 47 minutes, but his most noteworthy bouts were the three meetings with Bendigo. He lost the first in July 1835 after twenty-two rounds. The second confrontation saw Bendigo disqualified in the seventy-fifth round for dropping without a blow. In the third encounter in 1845 Caunt was disqualified for the same reason after ninety-three rounds.

This particular bust is impressed on the back ' By H. Bentley + Modeled from Life + 1844' (indented capitals). Bentley was a designer and manufacturer from Hanley. Caunt is shown bare-headed with fringe beard, high collar, bow tie, coat and waistcoat. Below the title indented capitals, 'Belt presented at Jem Burns May 1841'. The belt is modelled on the pedestal, along with details of Caunt's birth, height and weight and a list of his fights. Another example with the same modeller's mark but in a brown glaze is described as a Doulton stoneware figure. It measures $13\frac{3}{4}$ inches.

An even earlier fighter was James Figg who is generally acknowledged as the first champion of the English prize-ring. Born at Thame, he opened a school of arms in London known as Figg's Amphitheatre. The fate of the title was decided by three fights against Ned Sutton of Gravesend, all of which Figg won, retaining the championship from 1719 until 1730 and retiring unbeaten. Four years later he died. A print exists after the painting by Hogarth. There are also eighteenth-century mezzotints showing Figg stripped to the waist ready for action, and Jack Broughton in sparring pose.

It was Figg who discovered Broughton, who became known as the 'father of boxing'. He was unquestionably the finest bare-knuckle prize fighter and became champion in 1734 when he beat George Taylor at Tottenham Court Road, London in 20 minutes, but it is for other things that he is remembered. He invented boxing gloves and was responsible for the first code of rules to govern boxing. They were drawn up in

Very rare pottery plaque of the classic fight between Tom Spring and John Langan at Chichester on June 8th, 1824.

1743 and recognised until superseded by the London Prize-Ring Rules of 1838. There is an excellent mezzotint of John Broughton by J. Faber. Broughton died in 1789 aged eighty-five and was buried at Lambeth, when the pall-bearers – at his request – were the pugilists Mendoza, Ward, Ryan, Big Ben and Johnson.

Even earlier references to boxing are the wood-engravings from the *De Arte Gymnastica* of Hieronymus Mercurialis published in 1573. These show the vicious thongs (caestus) that were bound round the hands and forearms. They make knuckle-dusters look effeminate for the caestus were studded with sharp-pointed pieces of iron. A full-blooded blow from such a fist must have meant death in the Roman arena.

The year 1824 was a good one for the prize-ring. It saw two famous fights between Tom Spring, champion of England, and Jack Langan, the Irish title-holder. The first bout took place on 7 January at Worcester racecourse, in spite of opposition from the magistrates. An enormous crowd gathered; the stands were packed, whilst many used the riggings of boats anchored in the Severn as vantage-points. The fight had hardly begun when one of the stands collapsed and 2000 spectators fell with the wreckage. Once the injured were treated, the bout continued. After seventy-five punishing rounds, Langan was battered into submission. A

Single pottery plaque, also rare, of Tom Spring, protégé of Tom Cribb.

return match took place at Chichester on 8 June for a substantial stake of £500 a side. This time the ring was on a raised stage. A similar brusing fight ended after one hour and 48 minutes, when Langan fell senseless in the seventy-seventh round. Both fighters retired shortly afterwards. Langan left Cambridge, where he taught boxing to under-graduates, and became landlord of a tavern in Leicester Square (later the home of Tom Sayers). He died on 1 September 1871. Spring became landlord of the Castle Tavern in Holborn.

Both fighters are commemorated in striking fashion. A rare collector's piece is a fine Staffordshire boxing plaque of rectangular shape, with moulded black border, transfer-printed in black with Spring and Langan standing with bare fists raised, wearing breeches tied at the knees with bows, and a crowd of onlookers in the background. The plaque measures 16 ins × 13 ins. Smaller individual plaques were also made, as an attractive pair.

A coloured print on a Staffordshire lustre jug shows Spring fighting Langan in a raised ring, with both seconds inside the ropes and spec-tators in foreground and background. The caption reads: *Spring Champion of Great Britain*. Quite superb is a two-handled tankard 6 ins high and the same circumference. Spring and Langan are shown in realistic detail shaping-up for a fight. The vessel is gold rimmed and has gold on the base, with brown stakes and ropes on green-shaded grass. The wooded background is lanscaped with mansion, outbuilding and hay stacks against a salmon-pink skyline. Inside is a detailed rural frieze showing realistic models of frogs and lizards, the idea being that as the contents were consumed so the creatures were revealed. This particular mug is uncommon and a rarity for any collector.

The coloured print of the fight between Jack Randall, the Irishman whom George Borrow named as King of the Light-weights, and Martin the baker, provides the clearest detail of the background to a bout in 1818. The narrative caption records the progress of every round until the Irishman knocked out his heavier opponent after 50 minutes 10 seconds. Randall also figures in another coloured print drawn from life and etched by Williams. It depicts a straightforward fight against Be-lasco, the Jewish champion, that took place at Shepperton-Point near Oatlands on 30 September 1817 for 50 guineas a side. Randall gained the decision with this compliment: 'The Morning Chronicle, Bells Weekly Dispatch, Duckets and other Newspapers state this fight to have been on both sides the finest display of science and bodily activity witnessed for many years.'

John Martin is the subject of an individual print published in 1819, the caption giving a brief resumé of his fighting career. Richard Curtis received similar treatment in 1821. In both cases the stance adopted is that of a southpaw. There are several prints of John Gully, a remarkable personality who was bought out of a debtors' prison to become champion of England in 1807, became landlord of the Plough Inn, Carey Street, London, won a fortune on gambling, served as a Member of Parliament, owned a colliery, won the Derby three times, also the Two Thousand Guineas, and was offered a knighthood but declined. A rare print shows him fighting Hen Pearce, the 'Game Chicken', in a bout lasting sixty-four rounds and 1 hour 17 minutes. The verdict went against Gully who was outclassed by a more experienced fighter. A more dignified study of Gully is an engraving of the oil painting by Ben Marshall in 1810 which is on a par with this artist's treament of 'Gentleman' Jackson, champion of England 1795–1803. In this case Marshall has added in the background a framed painting of two pugilists stripped to the waist in contrast to Jackson's formal garb.

There is no doubt Jackson exercised considerable influence on the sport, opened a boxing school in Bond Street, London which was frequently patronised by Lord Byron. He was one of eighteen pugilists, including Cribb and Spring, who acted as bodyguards at the entrances to Westminster Hall at the coronation of King George IV. It is difficult to imagine a more formidable bunch of chuckers-out.

Of general interest are two prints of a panoramic caricature, *Road to a Fight*, divided into six studies depicting all walks of life making their way to the scene, the different types of conveyances, mishaps and incidents, finally showing the fight in progress with top-hatted officials and large crowd. Ackermann's published a similar treatment of the *Road to Epsom and the Derby* in 1851. This depicts the usual incidents on the way to Epsom, with the crowd departing from the Elephant and Castle and the actual race. This particular caricature is signed H.A., which might have been the combined work of the family of Henry Alken. The boxing studies cannot claim such an eminent origin, but the effect is just as entertaining.

Entirely different is a silk commemorative scarf with printed centre-piece showing Jem Mace, Champion of the World, surrounded by the championship belts of America, England, and Australia, the whole contained in a thick rope border, symbolic of the boxing ring. It measures 90 × 83 cm and is dated about 1890. Mace was the last of the old school of prize fighters and the father of current scientific boxing. Like W.G. Grace and J.H. Taylor in other sports, he lived long enough to see the transition. The closing years of his life saw him take a travelling circus round the country. It had a boxing and wrestling booth. In 1911 he came to Liverpool and pitched a site in Sefton Park. Whilst there, Mace became ill and had to be left behind when the circus moved on. He was taken to a Liverpool hospital, where he died aged seventy-nine and was

Optimistic verses on the reverse side of a jug that depicts the Molineux and Cribb fight.

buried in Anfield Cemetery. On a visit I tried to locate the grave. Sadly it is indicated only by a sandstone marker showing its number, 594. The memory of 'The Swaffham Gipsy', one of the cleverest of boxers, has slipped into obscurity except for the discerning collector.

The prize-ring of the eighteenth century was marked by displays of vicious almost barbaric cruelty. Broughton's Rules were respected in London and the Home Counties, but in the North nothing was barred. The sport as such was a mockery of the name. There was enthusiasm from the public, but champions were scarce. The turning-point came with Daniel Mendoza, the first Jewish boxer of consequence. Born in Aldgate in 1764 among the poverty of the East End, he had his first fight at the age of sixteen, developing into an outstanding scientific fighter. Subtlety and craft helped him to become Champion of England, and during that reign he had four memorable fights with Richard Humphrey. The first, in importance, was little better than a tavern quarrel at the Cock in Epping, but it set the tone for the next three contests. No love was lost between the two men. This was shown at Odiham in Hampshire when a fight that lasted less than half an hour ended with Mendoza being unable to continue because of a strained leg. Some 10,000 spectators headed by the Prince of Wales and the Duke of York, who had wagered £40,000 on the result, were treated to a remarkable display of skill and speed. Afterwards Humphreys wrote to his backer, 'Sir, I have done the Jew, and am in good health. – Richard Humphreys.' The next year, 1789, Humphreys was soundly thrashed by Mendoza at Stilton in Huntingdonshire. The final clash took place at Doncaster, when after seventy-two rounds of fierce fighting, Humphreys fell exhausted and the Jew was unquestionably the champion, a title he held until beaten by John Jackson at Hornchurch in 1795, the purse being 200 guineas a side.

The collector can look for several prints. Most famous is the one drawn by C.R. Ryley, engraved by J. Grozer, bearing the caption, 'This Boxing Match took place at Doncaster Sept 29th, 1790 on a Twenty four foot Stage and was the third Public Contest between these two pugilists. It lasted for about an Hour & five Minutes & was decisive in favour of Mendoza.' Another coloured engraving by T. Grozer after R. Einsle shows the Humphreys–Mendoza match at Odiham in January 1788, the colours and details being excellent.

Two individual studies were printed. A coloured print by J. Gillray shows Mendoza in a fighting pose described by Fewtrell: it 'is formed by the fists placed nearer each other, almost opposite to the chin, the left a little before the right; the legs not far removed, the left somewhat before, and the weight of the body on the foremost leg. Here the blow must be weaker, because there is loss of weight to propel it.' An interesting style analysis that is not entirely confirmed by the print. The second study is a mezzotint by J. Young of Richard Humphreys that was made from a painting by Hoppner for Wilson Braddyll, Humphrey's patron. Fewtrell tried another analysis, this time more accurate: 'consists in placing the left hand foremost, the fist to the mouth; the right hand nearer to the body, the fist covering the stomach; the legs considerably extended; the left foremost, the weight of the body poised on the right, and the head erect. This position is the most graceful I have ever seen, the head, the breast, the arms, the legs, are truly picturesque, and combine to improve each other. It is also the most manly; the breast expanded, the head boldly raised, and the limbs firmly planted, express the most martial air.'

A rare collector's piece is a mug showing a fight in progress between Humphreys and Mendoza. The design is transfer-printed and coloured over in red, green, yellow and puce. In addition to the fighters, the umpires and seconds are featured, with a key to the print in scrolls. A copy is in the Schreiber Collection in the Victoria and Albert Museum.

An attractive model of Bob Fitzsimmons in a pugilistic attitude commemorates his epic title fight in 1897 against James J. Corbett which ended with the Englishman becoming heavyweight champion of the world, the only one to do so under Queensberry Rules. So little is known of this man of iron constitution that the pottery figure is a rare addition to any collection.

A former British light-heavyweight champion once said to me, 'If ever you find yourself in Cornwall, be sure to visit the birthplace of Bob Fitzsimmons in Helston.' I remembered the advice. At the top of Wendron Street I found a little house that looked mildly surprised at having a tablet over the doorway bearing the inscription that under its roof had been born a future champion of the world. I stood on the second step and knocked on the door. It was opened by Mrs Coles who, with a rich Cornish accent, invited me inside.

'No, I've never seen a boxing match in my life,' she said, 'except when I was a little child I sneaked into the Salvation Army Hall to watch a scrap. I was too small to see anything, but my mother caught me and gave me a boxing match of my own.'

Behind the door I found a newspaper cutting showing Fitzsimmons in action.

'Upstairs is the room where he was born,' continued Mrs Coles. I thought of the scene in Carson City on St Patrick's Day 1897, when 20,000 people invaded the gold-rush township to watch the title fight between 'Gentleman Jim' Corbett, Heavyweight Champion of the World, and the Cornishman, Bob Fitzsimmons. In many ways Fitzsimmons was a freak. He had tremendous shoulders, a superb chest, but looked ungainly and awkward with knock-knees, spidery legs, and a peculiar build. The top-heavy body was not an object of beauty, but his stamina was exceptional. The Cornish blacksmith was tough to the point of being impervious to punishment.

The title fight lived up to its name. There were no shared purses. Both men signed an agreement to fight to a finish with the world title and £4000 at stake. The winner was to take all. The fight was historic for another reason. It was the first at which moving pictures were taken. Kinetoscope recorded it round by round. Pre-fight incidents were numerous. Special armed constables were at each entrance as Senators, hobos, Assemblymen, Indians from the reservation camp, gold miners, Chinese and negroes packed the arena. Everyone was searched, all weapons were confiscated. The fight had the additional novelty of being between two men who were sworn enemies outside the ring. They had almost staged a non-title scrap in a hotel lobby, whilst a campaign of vituperation had been carried on in a newspaper column.

In his ring-corner the Cornishman never once glanced at his opponent. The American decided that as defending champion he should offer to shake the hand of his challenger. Fitzsimmons ignored the gesture.

The fight provided a study in contrasts. Cool and calm, with the perfectly proportioned body of an athlete, Corbett was the orthodox boxer. In the opening seconds of the first round his left stabbed through the Cornishman's guard to the chin, followed by a stinging right to the ribs, then, in a flash, he was out of range. Fitzsimmons was too slow. His spidery legs could not match the side-stepping, bobbing, weaving Corbett. Time and again his flailing arms hit the air.

In cold-blooded fashion Fitzsimmons was being ripped and gashed to near-insensibility. At the end of five rounds only courage kept him on his feet. The cynical, mocking smile of 'Gentleman Jim' so infuriated him that he seemed incapable of fighting scientifically. All he wanted was wipe the mocking expression off the American's face. In the sixth round a wicked left hook to the chin floored the Cornishman. He rose at the count of nine, but all seemed over. The fists of the champion pulverised the swaying figure. Seldom has a fighter shown such courage.

The seventh round saw Fitzsimmons blasted from ring-post to ropes. Every now and then he was smashed, quivering, to the canvas. A vicious upper-cut severed an artery in his lip, and blood, like a red snake, coiled out of the Cornishman's mouth. It was at this moment that Fitzsimmon's wife, who was sitting by the ringside, began to scream advice which later became a fistic tag.

'Hit him in the slats, Bob!' she screamed. 'You'll never hit his head.'

Fitzsimmons heard the words. He half-stepped back and drove a tremendous right, well back and deep into Corbett's unprotected left side.

From that moment the Cornishman's strength slowly turned the scales in his favour. The cynical smile disappeared from Corbett's lips. By the fourteenth round the American had almost been chopped in two by Fitzsimmons's harpooning body attack. His eyes were glazed with the punishment he had taken. Corbett had burnt out the remnants of his strength. They broke from a clinch and the end came abruptly.

The Cornish market-town of Helston is proud to be the birthplace of Bob Fitzsimmons, the only Englishman to win the world heavyweight championship.

Fitzsimmons stepped in and drove a short left clean to the stomach. It was a punch that became world famous as the 'solar plexus'. Corbett, eyes heavy-lidded, threw up his hands, his body shaking. Very methodically, like a man drawing a bow, Fitzsimmons smashed a right to the jaw. The punch was unnecessary. The title had literally changed hands when the left glove was buried in the American's midriff. In agony on the canvas, Corbett tried to heave himself upright to beat the count, but collapsed, semi-paralysed.

I am sure that Mrs Coles would have fainted had she seen that fight in Carson City but, thinking only of her own juvenile experience in the Salvation Army Hall, she keeps fresh the triumph of Bob Fitzsimmons, the only Englishman to gain that elusive world heavyweight title.

The last great bare-knuckles fight of the prize-ring and the first international heavyweight contest was that between John Heenan and Tom Sayers at Farnborough, Hampshire on 17 April 1860. Heenan, known as 'The Benecia Boy'', claimed the American heavyweight title when John Morrissey retired in 1859, came to England and challenged our champion, Sayers. The fight was arranged even though it looked one-sided. The American dwarfed his opponent by six inches and had a weight advantage of three stone. Arrangements had to be secret so that the police had no knowledge of the venue. *The Times* of 2 April carried this paragraph:

> 'The Forthcoming Prize-Fight. – Hertford, Saturday. This afternoon Colonel Archibald Robertson, chief constable of the Hertfordshire Police Force, made application to the justices assembled in petty session at Hertford for a warrant to apprehend Thomas Sayers, the "Champion of England", and John Heenan, the American pugilist, in order that they might be bound over to keep the peace ...'

The attempt failed. A special train left London Bridge Station at 4 am carrying some thousand spectators to join a crowd of several thousand already gathered in a meadow where ditches and double hedges gave a measure of protection if the fighters had to leave in a hurry. The fight itself was brutal even by current standards. In the fifth round Sayers dislocated his right arm. For the next thirty-seven rounds it was useless, but the Englishman administered telling punishment with left piledrivers. Heenan, bleeding heavily, managed to get Sayers's neck caught by the top rope and threw his massive weight on it. The Englishman, black in the face, was on the verge of death when the umpires cut the ropes. Both men were almost battered to insensibility when the fight was abandoned through the arrival of the police. Heenan managed to reach the train, collapsed and was in a coma for several days in his London room. Sayers, although knocked to the ground more than twenty times, made a quicker recovery. The result was declared a draw after forty-two rounds lasting 2 hours 20 minutes. A champion's belt was awarded to each man. The *Cornhill* summarised the affair by saying that as prize fighting was illegal, the Queen could send her subject, Tom Sayers, to the treadmill for a month – and then knight him as he came out of prison.

Understandably there were several commemorative reminders of this fight. A print engraved by J.B. Rowbotham depicts the fight with an odd touch in that half the spectators are standing with their backs to the action for the benefit of the artist. Two excellent engravings show both boxers in sitting poses with realistic likenesses. Very rare is the panoramic engraving of Sayers's funeral procession which proceeded in state to Highgate Cemetery. On the print even Sayers's dog has a place to himself. He is sculptured in rough under the inscription of Sayers's name on the tomb. Most popular is the Staffordshire group titled *Heenan & Sayers* in raised capitals, showing both boxers bare to the waist in fighting pose. They wear breeches and long stockings. Two plain posts are in the background. It is interesting to examine the statuette of Tom Sayers in fistic pose by A. Bezzi which is in the National Portrait Gallery, London. Occasionally reproductions can be found.

Not all boxing ephemera belong to the past. Among the items is a limited edition of a bronze of Henry Cooper, 20 inches high, in a familiar crouching pose ready for action. It is an excellent likeness of this popular personality who created a record by holding the British heavyweight title for over ten years. The same can be said of the action figure of Muhammad Ali in a limited edition of 500 by Andrew Dishington.

The bibliography of the sport offers a wide range of titles, with such volumes as *Boxiana* by Pierce Egan (1818–24) and *Fistiana* by F. Dowling (1840) at the top of the list. Occasionally a blow-by-blow printed account can be found such as *The Championship of England* between Tom Sayers and the Benicia Boy dated 1860. Choice collector's items must include the early japanned Bilston snuff-boxes with fine painted enamels showing fistic bouts watched by top-hatted spectators. A fun item is an engraved metal circular tobacoo box bearing a boxing scene on the cover and with a secret compartment depicting activity that Mary Whitehouse might not approve of, but doubtless has entertainment value.

CHAPTER 10

SPORTS PHILATELY

Sports philately can be dated from the end of the last century. It began when Greece issued a series marking the first Olympic Games of the modern era, staged at Athens in 1896. All twelve stamps had conventional classical designs. Ten years later the same country produced a fresh series of fourteen stamps to celebrate the Olympic Games anniversary, again in Athens. Belgium broke fresh ground in 1920 with three special stamps commemorating the Olympic Games in Antwerp, but still stayed faithful to a classical design which persisted four years later when France, Costa Rica and Uruguay released new stamps. It was not until 1925 that this tradition was broken. Modern-designed sports stamps were issued by Hungary, not for any special occasion, but for sport generally with a surcharge of 100 per cent.

The innovation appealed. In the 1930s over a hundred sports stamps appeared. The war years halted the output, but it revived from the 1948 Olympic Games onwards. The 1950s had an annual average of 100 issues increasing to more than 300 new sports stamps in 1960. Thematic collecting had arrived in a big way and has never looked back. Designs have become more imaginative. Not only events but personalities have been recorded in sufficient numbers to justify specialised collections of individual sports. One way is to take country by country and arrange in chronological order which would give a record of design and format development. A more informal approach is to narrow the range to single outstanding sporting personalities. In that way it is possible to build up a gallery of historic interest. The following are but a few of the notable figures that have been commemorated on stamps: Emil Zatopek and his wife Dana Zatopkova on Czech stamps in 1954 and 1955; the hurdler J. Arifon of France on a stamp from Monaco; Baron de Coubertin, who founded the International Olympic Games

First Day Cover, autographed by the Kent players, that speaks for itself.

Committee in 1894 appears on three stamps of Haiti in 1939 and on a French stamp in 1956; Diagoras from Rhodes, a boxing champion in 464 BC, is on a Greek stamp of 1937. The designers used their imagination. The Olympic victor is shown being carried by his two sons Damagetos (pancration) and Akusitaos (champion boxer) at the 83rd Olympic Games of 448 BC; the Dynamo football team appeared on Russian stamps of 1948 and 1949; Vladimir Kuts, Victor Chukarin and Irene Jaunzeme were also featured by the Soviets after the 1957 Olympic Games at Melbourne; a rare sporting stamp comes from Colombia which in 1935 depicted the 5000-metres clash between J. Bouin of France and H. Kolehmainen of Finland in the 1912 Olympics.

Central America began the sequence of current sporting figures. Here are a few names at random: Terry Spinks, Mildred Zaharias, Fanny Blankers-Koen, Lord Burghley, Jesse Owens, Alain Mimoun, Paavo

First Day Cover of the 1968 Open Championship showing the historic trophy. The blank winner's space was Gary Player.

Nurmi, Chris Brasher, Shirley Strickland, Hans Winkler, Carlo Pavesi, and so on. Recent issues from various countries include Cassius Clay, Larry Holmes, Bobby Jones, Gary Sobers, the World Cricket Cup when the West Indies won in 1975. Guyana produced an interesting cricket set to mark the MCC tour of the West Indies in 1968: Andy Roberts, Ranji, Viv Richards are featured in an Antigua issue along with a group photograph of the West Indian champions. Bermuda produced a fine series of their cricket grounds to mark the 75th anniversary Cricket Cup matches.

First Day Covers are also well worth collecting and there are some choice examples. There is the Medallic First Day Cover issued by the Test and County Cricket Board to celebrate *County Cricket 1873–1973*. *Kent County Cricket Club Centenary 1870–1970*, a commemorative First Day Cover posted on St Lawrence Ground, Canterbury on 30 May

Every year Monaco produces special issues marking the Grand Prix of Monaco,
usually featuring racing and vintage cars.

1970, bears the signatures of Kent players like Colin Cowdray, Derek
Underwood, John Shepherd and Alan Knott. The official Cover for the
200th running of the Derby on 6 June 1979 bears the reproduced
painting by Katherine Welsh which shows in the background the fair
at Tattenham Corner, and at the winning post the colours of four
famous Derby winners; Sea Bird, Nijinsky, Mill Reef and Royal Palace.
The Post Office also marked the Derby 200 milestone with a special
issue of horseracing stamps. Sir Alfred Munnings's painting of Mahmoud at Epsom is reproduced. Owned by the Aga Khan, this horse won
in 1936 in the record time of 2 mins 33·8 secs (over 35 mph). The
other three stamps of this issue show the First Spring Meeting at Newmarket in 1793; Racing at Dorsett Ferry, Windsor in 1684; and the
Liverpool Grand National Steeple Chase of 1839.

In golf the Open Championship of 1968 at Carnoustie inspired a
Commemorative Cover posted on the final day showing the famous
Trophy that has been a challenge since 1872. On the base of the

envelope is given past winners at this championship links; Jose Jurado in 1931, Henry Cotton over a gale-lashed links against the cream of American invaders in 1937, Ben Hogan with machine-like precision in 1953. The year of the Commemorative Issue saw Gary Player succeed. The Championship returned to Carnoustie in 1975 when Tom Watson took the Trophy back to America in his luggage. A personalised First Day Cover appeared on 17 August 1970 marking Stanley Matthews's first home match for Blackpool back in Division One. The postage stamp marked England's victory in the World Cup of 1966; it shows in detail Matthews with the ball at his feet, and records his eighty-four international appearances for England, and the dates – Blackpool FC (1947–61), (FA Cup 1953), and Stoke City (1961–1965). The World Football Championship of 1966 also had a separate Cover with stamps showing players in action. Rugby League had a striking Commemorative Cover when St Helens' Saints won the Challenge Cup at Wembley in 1972, with the players looking formidable and determined in their distinctive strip.

Outstanding among First Day Covers must be the official Test Cricket Commemorative issued by the Australian Cricket Board in a strictly limited edition combining a sterling silver proof medal with the five stamps honouring the Centenary of Test Cricket 1877–1977 and officially postmarked at the Melbourne Cricket Ground on 15 March 1977, exactly one hundred years after the first day's play. The stamps perhaps lack the delight touch brought by Harry Furniss to his drawings of W.G. Grace on the occasion of the County Cricket Centenary, but are nevertheless a rare addition to any thematic collection.

VANITY FAIR PRINTS

Vanity Fair cricket prints offer scope to the would-be collector who is deterred by the inflated prices of almost everything of specialised interest. Here is a vintage line-up of highly personal caricatures and stylised images which form a graphic commentary of a past age of the game.

Vanity Fair, the creation of Thomas Gibson Bowles, was published every week between November 1868 and January 1914. Acid comments and pertinent caricatures made the journal the Victorian equivalent of *Private Eye* with barbs directed at society, politics, fashion and the social background to contemporary Victorian and Edwardian life. The section 'Men of the Day' gave ample scope for caustic comment by Bowles, ably supported by trenchant colour cartoons by Carlo Pellegrini, under the pseudonym Singe, later changed to Ape; Leslie Ward contributed from 1873 and was better known by his pseudonym, Spy. Max Beerbohm also contributed in a style influenced by Pellegrini, whilst W.R. Sickert was persuaded to add his work from time to time. Their cartoons became a topic of national comment. Every study carried biographical notes from the trenchant pen of Bowles under the nom de plume of Jehu Junior. In all more than 2000 cartoons were published mirroring the frivolities, eccentricities and vanities of high society, a social commentary of considerable interest.

In such volatile company, cricketers were dull by comparison and as such were neglected. It was nine years before the first cricket cartoon was published on 9 June 1877. Appropriately the choice was *Dr William Gilbert Grace* who, at that time, exercised immense influence on the game. Depicted in cricketing attire, the treatment is somewhat wooden, but it marked the recognition of the game as part of the English scene. The second cartoon, published on 13 July 1878, was the Australian

Frederick Robert Spofforth, the 'Demon Bowler', who made the headlines by taking 10 wickets for 20 runs against an England side that included Grace. That in itself justified recognition. Jehu Junior added his comments, 'He is withal of excellent manners, modest, and diffident, and has become a favourite with all who have known him in England. One of his sisters married a brother of Lady Lyttelton, whose step-sons are considered by the Australian cricketers to be the finest batsmen they have encountered since their arrival in England.'

The name of *George Bonnor* is comparatively unknown, but this sturdy Australian amateur made a lasting impression. The cartoon by Ape in 1884 emphasised his physical fitness which was confirmed in the biographical notes ... 'His father was from Herefordshire, his mother was from Lancashire, and he was born eight-and-twenty years ago at Bathhurst in New South Wales. He was sent to school and he went into the Bush, attached himself to sheep-farming and learnt to shoot, to ride, and to run, and has now come back to his Mother-country to represent Australian cricket as one of the Australian Eleven. He is a quiet, amiable, low-voiced, comely giant, standing six feet six in his boots, measuring forty-five inches round the chest, and weighing seventeen stone all but two pounds. He has thrown a cricket-ball 129 yards. He can bowl very fast indeed, and is a very hard hitter. He is a fine runner too, and is the hundred yards champion of New South Wales. He is neither a smoker nor a drinker, he is gentle and good-humoured, and is altogether a most excellent specimen of the Greater Briton.'

Bonnor's playing record in England fell short of this fulsome pen-portrait. In the first Test of 1880 against Lord Harris's side that included three Grace brothers, the Australian clouted a ball so high that they ran three runs before being caught by G.F. Grace. This first Test match to be played in England was highlighted by W.G. Grace who made 152, the Australian captain, W.L. Murdoch, bettered it by one run. The third Grace brother, Fred, collected a brace in his only Test appearance, tragically dying a fortnight later from pneumonia at the age of twenty-nine. Bonner did not shine. England won by five wickets, the captain, *Lord Harris* was the subject for a Spy cartoon.

Ape caricatured the likeness of the *Hon. Alfred Lyttleton* in the issue of *Vanity Fair* for 20 September 1884. The notes read; 'Mr Lyttelton is the eighth son of the late Lord Lyttelton. He was born seven-and-twenty years ago, and is an excellent young man of good manners and of good report. By profession he is a barrister, and, as such, is second 'Devil' to the present Attorney-General, who honours him with especial confidence. It is, however, as one of the lights of English Cricket that he is best known, and especially as a wicket-keeper. He is considered one of the best of the amateur players. He is very popular. He recently lost his overcoat.'

Four years later appeared a stolid cartoon of *Walter William Read*, a name that means little to most people. Jehu Junior had similar thoughts, '... the reason that so little is known of Mr Read's early life is probably the fact that there is nothing about it worth knowing'. Nevertheless he gave yeoman service to Surrey, heading the batting averages twelve times with a memorable partnership with W.E. Roller against Lancashire in 1887 which produced 305. The biographical notes gave more detail. 'Mr Read is quite one of the best bats in the world. He plays very straight and hits all round with much freedom, so that no amateur Eleven is now complete without him. His off-drives are unequalled, and the way in which he lengthens a "long hop" on the off, sending it between point and mid-off with the speed of a round shot, is a thing to be seen and not forgotten. He can keep wicket with the best of them, and though, in order to save his hands for batting, he does not always do so, he once kept it for Surrey while the Yorkshire Eleven scored 388 runs, without allowing them a single extra.' Read was a man of many roles. 'He is an Association footballer of some reputation, and has won prizes for walking. He can skate well, and nurse billiard balls as few amateurs can nurse them. He is very popular with the Proletariat, which speaks of him familiarly as "Walter", though he is more widely known as "W.W." He is or has been, a master in a select academy. He is also said to be something in the City.' Altogether W.W. must have been a rare all-rounder to justify *Vanity Fair* treatment.

The same might be said about *Hylton Philipson*. He is shown by Spy in cricket garb, but the editor was not over-impressed. 'He is not a great batsman and he cannot bowl; but he does well behind the sticks in a position in which it is a great advantage for a captain to be.' When Spy executed his cartoon, Philipson was Oxford captain of an Eleven that

(*opposite*): *Spy* likeness of Tom Hayward, famed for first wicket stands with Jack Hobbs, including 352 against Warwickshire in 1909 and 313 against Worcester.

105

was struggling. 'Notwithstanding successive defeats, he is full of hope for the big match at Lord's.' It was wishful thinking, for Cambridge won by an innings and 105 runs. To portray him in cricketing garb at this point in his playing career was perhaps flattery, but he was versatile, became Amateur Rackets Champion, did well at football, played cricket for Middlesex, but possibly was featured on the basis of his social background of a Scottish castle and legal career.

A.N. Hornby earned his place by skill not social graces. This son of a Blackburn mill-owner made his mark as Lancashire captain. In 1881 the side gained the championship with an unbeaten record and Hornby topping the battling averages. He was involved in the controversy over Crossland, whose bowling action was suspect after claiming eleven wickets in one match. Hornby did not agree the delivery was unfair. In 1897 he came out of retirement, took MacLaren's place as captain and had the satisfaction at the age of fifty to bring the championship to Lancashire by winning the title outright.

Andrew Ernest Stoddart was a great favourite at Lord's and an all-rounder, playing rugby for England between 1885 and 1893 and the Barbarians in 1890–1. The biographical note records that 'he is so keen upon the game that he has been known to save himself for a big match by staying in bed until it was time to take the field'. In cricket he was a powerful batsman and a useful change bowler. In the cartoon he is shown in Queen's Club colours.

The cartoon of *S.M.J. Woods* is interesting, for this double Cambridge blue had the unusual distinction of representing both England and Australia at cricket. The notes declare that 'he has taken so kindly to English ways that he is now engaged in learning to make beer in a Somersetshire brewery'. The Australian is described as 'good-tempered, bullet-headed ... and can speak his mind'.

The study of Lord Hawke by Spy looks too bland and innocuous. This dour cricketer was a disciplinarian, captained Yorkshire from 1883 to 1910, won the County Championship eight times, and led touring sides in 154 matches, losing only 13. The biographical notes end with the postscript, 'He is a member of the Carlton and the Bachelors', good-looking, pleasant, modest fellow: and though he is not as yet a great statesman he is a good Conservative'.

Charles Burgess Fry is shown by Spy in athletic gear with the caption 'Oxford Athletics', but such was his versatility the choice was wide. He was one of the finest all-round sportsmen England has produced. His cricketing record speaks for itself – over 30,000 runs with an average of 50. In 1901 he made 3147 runs including six successive centuries. He captained Oxford, the Gentlemen, and England in the Triangular Tests with his sides unbeaten. His fast bowling earned two hat-tricks for Oxford against the MCC at Lord's. So much for cricket. He held the world record for the long jump; ran the hundred and jumped the high jump for Oxford; played for England at football; appeared in a Cup Final; stood for Parliament; represented India at Geneva; wrote Latin verses for *The Times*; beat Lord Birkenhead for a Wadham scholarship; was offered the throne of Albania; and managed in spite of these diverse activities to be the greatest run-scorer at a period of England's strongest players. The biographical note ends with the laconic 'He is generally liked,' possibly the understatement of all time.

Kumar Shri Ranjitsinhji is one of the gems of Spy cartoons. Here was the master of attacking strokes with a magical flowing movement, a cricketer on a par with W.G. Grace and Don Bradman. Ranji learnt his cricket at Rajkumar College in Kathiawar and perfected his style to such a degree that in all he scored 24,567 runs with an average of 45 and made 72 centuries, ten of them in 1896. His silk shirts were always buttoned at the wrist, a touch that Spy did not overlook. His feathered leg glances were the most delicate ever seen at Lord's.

Captain Edward Wynward is an unknown name, but important in that it comes into the *Vanity Fair* collection. A batsman of obvious skill, he scored three successive centuries for Hampshire in 1894. Jehu Junior added an odd postcript to his notes, 'He can speak his mind; and is supposed to think less of K.S. Ranjitsinhji than some of the public do.' Apparently the remark refers to an argument with Ranji over fruit at the dinner table.

There is no anonymity about *Gilbert Laird Jessop*. A fearless hitter with an unorthodox batting style in a characteristic crouch; six times he made a century in under an hour. Against the West Indies he made 157 runs in an hour, and in 75 minutes made a memorable 104 runs that gave England a one-wicket victory over Australia at the Oval. When he came to the wicket England were 48 for 5. When he was caught at short-leg only 77 were needed to win. As a fast bowler he took 851 wickets at an average of 22·91, and was an outstanding fielder at cover-point. The Spy cartoon does justice to the subject.

Digby Loder Armroid Jephson is another somewhat obscure player. He played for Surrey at the beginning of the century, a useful bat and confident lob bowler. He is recorded in the act of putting on 364 for the first wicket with Bobby Abel at the Oval, but the biographical notes tell more about the man than mere statistics. 'He is a nice-looking boy, who has contributed entertainingly to cricket literature. He has also confessed to missing a player through sleeping at extra slip: yet there is no risk of the depreciation of Surrey cricket while he is the Surrey Captain. They call him the 'Lobster', but he has his eccentricities. For he likes music and golf: and he has written a Fairy Tale.'

If Jephson was the lobster, *Bobby Abel* was the shrimp, though the nickname given was 'The Guv'nor'. He was not much bigger than his bat, at least so it seemed from the pavilion, but he produced some remarkable innings. At the Oval in 1899 he made 357 not out against Somerset and was at the wicket for $8\frac{1}{2}$ hours while 811 runs were amassed, and in the 1892 Test at Sydney he carried his bat through the innings for 132 not out. The Spy cartoon is a gem.

The study of *Frank Stanley Jackson* is good. The elegant touch of the cavalier moustache was part of the 'Jacker' approach. An orthodox batsman, right-hand fast-medium bowler and brilliant cover-point fielder, he was one of England's outstanding all-rounders. He was chosen to play for England while still a Cambridge undergraduate and scored 91 in his first Test innings against Australia at Lord's. His final tally was 15,782 runs for an average of 34·76, and 770 wickets for 20·28. He later became president of the MCC and chairman of the England Test Selectors in 1934.

Lionel Charles Hamilton Palairet is another shadowy figure from the past. A graceful cricketer who played in two Tests against Australia under the captaincy of Shrewsbury. The caption identifies him with Repton, Oxford and Somerset with the comment for extra weight that 'He is a good shot and a capital billiard player.'

The tubby figure of *George Hirst* was one of Yorkshire's greatest characters, even more so than fiery Freddie Trueman for not only was he a superb batsman scoring 36,203 runs with an average of 34·05, capturing 2727 wickets at only 18·77, but held 601 catches. His aggressive approach to the game came out in the 1902 Test at the Oval. The result was in the balance; 15 runs were needed. Wilfred Rhodes, last man in, came to the wicket. Hirst, who finished 58 not out, met

Wilfred and told him they would get the runs in singles, which is exactly what they did. The Spy cartoon is too bland for such a bustling professional.

Pelham Francis Warner stands out as the finest ambassador of the game. During a long life he served cricket in so many different ways. His debut for Middlesex was in 1894 and he was an active county player until the close of the 1920 season. As captain it was fitting that Middlesex should win the championship and that his own score in that last game with Surrey should be an immaculate 79. 'Plum's' personal tally was 60 centuries in first-class cricket, 32 of them being made at Lord's. His Test debut was in South Africa during the 1898–99 tour and was marked by an innings of 132 not out. He skippered England in the Australian series of 1903–4 and in South Africa in 1905–6. In 1897 and 1898 he led a team in America, and took one to Australia in 1911–12. For seven years he was chairman of the Test Selectors and President of the MCC in 1950. Seldom has a knighthood been so genuinely conferred for services to the game. The Spy cartoon shows him as a young cricketer, already showing a thinning thatch. As the biographical note concludes, 'He owes his wigmaker a bill.'

To many people the name Bosanquet suggests a man who used to read news bulletins on television. The connection is real. *Bernard James Tindal Bosanquet* was the father of the newscaster and a cricketer of rare distinction. At Eton his efforts at cricket, soccer and the wall game were those of a natural; his promise continued at Oriel where he collected a blue at cricket, half-blues for athletics and ice hockey, and became captain of university billiards and skipper of the Oriel soccer team. The only thing he failed to collect was a degree. He turned to cricket, played for Middlesex from 1898 to 1919, but his claim to fame rests on the introduction of the googly, a bowling variation that revolutionised the game. Chosen for the first MCC side to tour Australia, 'Bosie' came into his own in the third and fourth Tests. His novel googlies confused the Australians. At Adelaide he took 4 for 73, but in Sydney with the Australians needing 329, 'Bosie' claimed 5 for 12 at one stage, finished with 6 for 51, and England won the Ashes. In the Test at Nottingham in 1905 he struck again with a second innings analysis of 8 for 107. His son, Reginald, presented the ball used at Trent Bridge to the museum at Lord's.

Thomas Hayward, born at Cambridge, made his appearance for Surrey in 1893 and was bowled for a duck – a hesistant debut that became a long and distinguished association. As opening batsman and partner to Jack Hobbs, he took part in more than 40 stands of a century or more. In 1906 he made 2000 runs, including 10 centuries, by the first week of July. He first scored 1000 in a season in 1895 and repeated the feat every season until he retired in 1914. As a medium-pace bowler he took some 500 wickets in his career. He was the first batsman after W.G. Grace to record a century of centuries.

Spy produced a pleasing cartoon of *Reginald Herbert Spooner*, an all-rounder who played for Lancashire and England. In 1903 he played for England against Wales as wing three-quarter, played in ten Tests between 1905 and 1912, and had to decline the captaincy of the MCC touring side to Australia in 1920.

Another dour Lancastrian was *John Thomas Tyldesley*, of half-pint size with a remarkable ability to master unpredictable pitches. He scored 1000 runs in nineteen consecutive seasons, four times topped the 2000-mark and in 1901 amassed 3041. His top score was 295 not out against Kent in 1906 at Old Trafford. He played a major role in England's victory over Australia at Melbourne in 1904. In the first innings he made 97; in the second innings six of the first England batsmen made 10 runs between them. Tyldesley scored 62 out of 85.

The *Reverend F.H. Gillingham* was a cleric of varied tastes. The biographical notes added 'He is a fine preacher but his reputation on the cricket field gives him a better chance of saving souls than would all the eloquence in the world. He rides when he can get anything up to his weight. He fancies himself somewhat in his mess kit.' He toured the West Indies with Lord Tennyson's XI in 1927 and was Chaplain to King George VI.

C.M. Wells is another who may not be known, but he played for many years in the Middlesex XI, scoring 244 against Notts at Trent Bridge in 1899. *Vanity Fair* had a few pertinent notes: 'His flannels are bought by the yard and would keep two ordinary men warm even during the present wintry weather, and when the fifth catch has been dropped off his bowling his ejaculations are believed to be taken from Aristophanes.'

K.L. Hutchings was a doughty Kent batsman with a dashing style that stood him in good stead in the second Test at Melbourne in 1908 with an innings of 126 and Jack Hobbs 83 turned the scales for England by one wicket.

Colin Blythe was a superb left-hand bowler, taking an enormous tally of wickets for Kent. At Northampton he took 17 wickets for 48 runs, and on a South African tour under 'Plum' Warner he claimed 17 wickets for 48 runs – 10 for 30 in the first innings, and 7 for 18 in the second. The South Africans seemed to be favourite victims, for at Leeds in 1907 he took 8 for 59 and 7 for 40. Two years later he topped the averages against Australia and helped with Hirst to rout the Tourists for 74 in the first innings of the opening Test after bowling without a break.

The cartoon of *Jack Hobbs* does justice to the subject. He was a superb batsman under all types of conditions. His two-eyed stance and defensive back stroke was copied by many batsmen. Born at Cambridge, the eldest of twelve children, Hobbs tried to join Essex but was turned down, a decision that county rued for many a year. Surrey made no mistake. During his career that stretched from 1905 to 1934 he scored 61,237 runs for an average of 50·65, which included 197 individual centuries. He played in 61 Tests from the 1907–8 Australian tour to the final innings for England at the Oval against Australia in 1930. Four years earlier on the same ground he joined Sandham in a first-wicket stand of 428 against Oxford University. The same season against Middlesex at Lord's, Hobbs scored 316 not out. As a bowler his slow-medium pace was most effective. In 1920 he headed the averages. His last century in first-class cricket was in the George Duckworth Benefit match at Old Trafford, scoring 116 and 51 not out. He was then aged fifty-one. Hobbs was also a brilliant cover-point.

Another cartoon is that of *Edward Wentworth Dillon*, who led Kent to several championship titles after accepting the captaincy in 1909. The biographical note sums up his approach to the game. 'He has a way of making a pair of spectacles and has accomplished this feat twice this season. But he is still fonder of making a 'duck' in the first innings and a century in the second. This is almost a hobby with him.'

As a collection these cartoons form a fine assembly of historic cricketers making a graphic commentary on the principal figures in an age that encouraged 'characters'. They capture the spirit of that period. As a guide to anyone who intends to collect them, the following is a list with the dates when they were published in *Vanity Fair:*

W.G. Grace . . . .   9 June 1877.
F.R. Spofforth . . . .   13 July 1878.
G.J. Bonnor . . . .   13 September 1884.
Hon. A. Lyttleton . . . .   20 September 1884.
W.W. Read . . . .   28 July 1888.
H. Philipson . . . .   29 June 1889
A.N. Hornby . . . .   15 August 1891.
A.E. Stoddart . . . .   9 July 1892
S.M.J. Woods . . . .   6 August 1892
Lord Hawke . . . .   24 September 1892
C.B. Fry . . . .   19 April 1894.
K.S. Ranjitsinhji . . . .   26 August 1897
Captain E. Wynward . . . . . .   25 August 1898.
G.L. Jessop . . . .   25 July 1901.
D.L.A. Jephson . . . .   22 May 1902.
Robert Abel . . . .   5 June 1902.
Hon. F.S. Jackson . . . .   28 August 1902.
L.C.H. Palairet . . . .   6 August 1903.
George Hirst . . . .   20 August 1903.
Pelham Warner . . . .   3 September 1903.
B.J.T. Bosanquet . . . .   15 September 1904.
T. Hayward . . . .   7 November 1906.
R.H. Spooner . . . .   18 July 1906.
J.T. Tyldesley . . . .   8 August 1906.
Reverend F.H. Gillingham . .   15 August 1906.
C.M. Wells . . . .   10 July 1907.
K.L. Hutchings . . . .   8 August 1907.
Colin Blythe . . . .   3 August 1910.
Jack Hobbs . . . .   19 August 1912.
E.W. Dillon . . . .   7 August 1913.
Lord Harris . . . .   16 July 1881.
J.L. Baldwin . . . .   5 September 1895.
Duke of Beaufort . . . .   30 August 1876.
C.C. Clarke . . . .   19 November 1896.
Lord Lyttleton . . . .   1 April 1871.
Hon. G.W. Spencer Lyttelton   4 December 1875.
6th Earl of Dartmouth . . . . .   10 October 1895.
R.A.H. Mitchell . . . .   16 July 1896.

C.F.C. Clarke	19 November 1896.
D.H. McLean	8 April 1897.
Maharaja of Patiala	4 January 1900.
Hon. N.G. Lyttelton	5 September 1901.
Reverend H.M. Burge	2 July 1903.
Reverend Dr J.C. Ryle	26 March 1881.
Earl of Darnley	7 April 1904.
Sir Spencer Ponsonby-Fane	26 January 1878.
Viscount Cobham	5 May 1904.
Lord Dalmeny	22 September 1904.
R.H.B. Marsham	12 October 1905.
E. Lubbock	4 January 1906.
Sir A.C. Lucas	6 February 1909.
Mr Justice Bray	27 October 1888.
Leslie Ward (Spy)	Men of the Day, No. 449, 1889.

COMMEMORATIVE MEDALLIONS

Over the last few years there has been a marked upsurge of interest in collecting medals commemorating sporting events at both national and international level. Although not extensive, this branch of numismatics is important. In time the medals will provide another dimension of sporting history in the style of their times. The obverse of a medal frequently bears a stylised portrait or scene, often by artists, who are not only medal designers but also painters or sculptors, and contemporary with the events and people portrayed. It is becoming an imaginative collecting field that has widened from the previous restricted range of Olympic and Commonwealth Games. In medals two things are to be considered, the Device and the Legend. The Device consists of figures or symbols, which should be perfectly well adapted to the occasion and intent of the medal. The Legend is a key or explanation to the Device, and should be apt, concise and clear. Medals thus contrived are descriptive, historical and instructive.

The Thomas Cribb Commemorative Medal is a rare reminder of the prize-fighting Champion of England and was issued in 1811 following his last fight against Molineux on 28 September of that year. It has the portrait of Cribb in an action pose with two posts and two ropes of the ring in the background. The reverse side shows a circular wreath of laurel leaves and the legend reads: 'Successful in 10 battles. The last Sept. 28th 1811 with Molineux at Thistleton Gap'.

An unusual medal was issued in 1822. The legend reads: The Sportsman's Delight: Blood; Bone; Action and Game'. It served as a membership token to a sports venue owned by Neat and Gas. The obverse side tells it all. In the centre is inset a square with a lion facing right. The sides of the square represent trimmed turf. At the top are two racehorses with jockeys, one using his whip; at the base two game cocks are fighting; on the right two dogs are scrapping; on the left there is bull-baiting with the bull being attacked by a dog with its owner in attendance. The reverse shows two prize-fighters in a scrap. The legend says: 'The good old English custom of deciding a quarrel'. Underneath in prominent letters: Neat and Gas.

Another early medal was struck in silver in 1837 to commemorate the founding of the National Swimming Society by John Strachan on 30 June of that year. The obverse side has a bust of John Strachan facing left with the legend 'John Strachan 1837'. The reverse has two swans in the water facing each other, with a child in between them resting an arm on the back of each swan. Above is the scroll 'Art and Confidence'. The legend states: 'National Swimming Society'.

Another rare medal struck in silver and bronze in 1861 commemorates the instruction of the first Army officer and twelve NCOs in physical training. The men, popularly known as The Apostles, were trained by Archibald Maclaren in the Oxford University gymnasium. From this course PT was introduced into the British Army. The obverse shows the Oxford University gymnasium with the legend, '*Mens sana in corpore sano*' (a healthy mind in a healthy body), the motto of the Army Physical Training Corps. The reverse has a circular belt and the words 'Oxford Gymnasium'. The names of the thirteen men are engraved on the edge of the medal: Major Frederick Hammersley, 14th Foot; Sgt Tarbottom, 5th Lancers; Sgt Reilly, 18th Hussars; Sgt Rafferty, 45th Foot; Sgt Steal, 32nd Foot; Sgt Kearney, 1/10th Foot; Sgt Bear, RA; Sgt Cox, 16th Lancers; Sgt Bartlett, RA; Sgt Jackson, 49th Foot; Sgt Flanaghan, 41st Foot; Sgt Smith, 55th Foot; Sgt Shepperd, RE.

Entirely different is the Calcutta Medal of 1892 issued by the Bombay Golf Club which was founded in 1842. The obverse shows a tropical scene with bending palms and two golfers resting beneath them, seeking shade from the visible rays of the sun. The winner of this prestigious event was J.C. Mason. The reverse has crossed long-nosed golf clubs with supporting garland and the captain's name: H.H. Glass, Esq. He it was who proposed at a meeting held in the Fort on 9 January 1842 that the Royal Bombay Gymkhana Golf Club be formed. This decision was noted in the Minutes of the Blackheath Club at a meeting held in the Green Man Hotel by referring to an announcement in the *Bombay Times*. 'It was resolved that the Blackheath Golf Club do immediately congratulate their countrymen on the formation of a Golfing Society at

Bombay, and transmit to them forthwith a copy of the Laws of the Game and the Regulations of the Blackheath Golf Club (believed to be the oldest Golfing Society in the Kingdom), with the expression of the Club's most anxious wishes for the prosperity and perpetuity of the Bombay Golf Club, and at the same time to intimate that the Captain of the said Club is, *ex officio*, an Honorary Member of the Blackheath Golf Club.'

The reply brought a similar invitation to the Field Marshal, Captain, Office Bearers and other members of the Blackheath Golf Club. Then in a later letter dated 2 October 1843, which was copied into the Minute Book. ... 'I sent you by the steamer of the 17 July, in charge of Lieut. Duncan of the Bengal Service, a Medal resolved by the Bombay Golf Club to be presented to their Blackheath Brethren, and by them bestowed as considered most expedient in testimony of the cementation of the treaty of eternal friendship betwixt the two august bodies. I have every reason to believe that this must have been lost on the occasion of the Wreck of the *Memnon*, from which no property whatever appears to have been saved.

'I am now once more directed to avail myself of the services of Colonel Cannan to carry to you another Medal, a duplicate of the former, and to request that you will do us the honour of presenting it to the Club.'

This was duly done and the Bombay Medal, bearing the same design with palm trees and reclining golfers, is one of this historic Clubs most prized medal trophies. There is a long list of past winners, beginning with Charles Sutherland in 1848.

The Bombay medal is but one of countless examples of historic medals held by famous golf clubs. The Royal and Ancient Club has a gold medal presented by King William IV in 1837 to be played for annually. Another is the attractive George Glennie Medal presented to the Club by Royal Blackheath in 1880. Another handsome gold medal contested on the first day of the Spring meeting of the Royal Liverpool Golf Club at Hoylake was bought by the members in 1870 for £70. Equally impressive is the Autumn Gold Medal of the Royal Burgess Golfing Society of Edinburgh which was founded in 1735. The Gold Medal of the Royal Aberdeen Golf Club first appeared in 1816. A more unusual medal is the Simpson Medal of the Honourable Company of Edinburgh Golfers presented by Sir Walter Simpson and played for at the same time as the Company's Gold Medal. The list could be lengthened. The originals can never be won outright, but collectable dated replicas can be found occasionally.

The Olympic Games provide many interesting medals. The first Games of the modern era were revived by Baron de Coubertin and held at Athens in 1896, Paris in 1900 and St Louis in 1904. The 1908 Games were scheduled for Rome but difficulties arose with the Italian Olympic Committee and the British Olympic Association was substituted. Two medals were designed by Bertram Mackennal a contemporary sculptor who was born in Melbourne, one for the successful athletes, the second a commemorative one for all competitors and officials. The obverse of the latter depicts an ancient chariot with two riders handling four horses. The reverse shows the winged figure of Fame holding an oak and laurel spray, the oak symbolising the sacred grove at Olympus, the laurel being the symbol of victory. A trumpet is held in the left hand. The legend reads: 'Elis, Athens, Paris, St Louis, London. In commemoration of the Olympic games held in London, 1908'. In 1948 the XIV Olympiad was held at the Empire Stadium, Wembley in London. The commemorative medal was produced by John Pinches. The obverse was the same as that of the 1908 Games, but the reverse showed Big Ben and St Stepehn's Tower at Westminster, with the five interlocked rings of the International Olympic Committee and the date.

Mexico 1968 and Munich 1972 produced interesting Olympic medals but Cecilia Leete excelled in her design for the 1984 Winter Olympics. This partical medal was the result of the Royal Society of Arts Design Bursaries Competition which has had a most important influence on the revival of medallic art. It was sponsored by the Goldsmiths Company, the Birmingham Mint and the Tower Mint with the shortlist dominated by students from the Jewellery Design Department at the Central School of Art.

The 1958 British Empire and Commonwealth Games at Cardiff produced a fine medal. The obverse has a 20-link chain around the outside with the Imperial Crown in the centre. The reverse has the Red Dragon of Wales in the centre facing left and standing on a curved riband with a Welsh leek on each side. In relief are action figures of nine athletes representing Running, Fencing, Rowing, Weight-lifting, Bowling, Cycling, Swimming, Boxing and Wrestling. The IX British Commonwealth Games at Edinburgh in 1970 had a simpler medal. The obverse had the Imperial Crown in the centre. The reverse had a lion rampant between

Tom Burgess who swam the Channel from England to France, September, 1911.

two thistle leaves surrounded by eight shields bearing alternately the diagonal cross of St Andrew and a Scottish thistle.

The year 1920 produced an unusual medal for the National Cross Country Championships. King George V gave permission for the event to be held in Windsor Great Park and the winners, Birchfield Harriers, were awarded a special medal to commemorate the occasion. Such medals would usually be regarded as winners' medals, but the rules stated that the winners should receive gold not silver medals. A second presentation therefore took place later, a gesture that gives the original silver medals a rare value. The obverse shows the head of King George V with the reverse reading National/Cross Country/Championship/at Windsor/March 13th 1920/ Winning Team.

The 1967 World Trampoline Championship at the Crystal Palace National Recreation Centre in 1967 produced a medal that showed on the obverse a trampoline at sideways angle with the twin hemispheres of the world in relief and a rhythmic line symbolising the movements made by the competitors.

Very rare is the commemorative medal marking the Cross-Channel swim by T.W. Burgess in 1911. The obverse shows the head of Burgess facing left, with the reverse carrying this legend in eleven horizontal lines: To/Commemorate/The Swim From/England to France/Sep 5–6 1911 by/T.W. Burgess/Presented by/Alfred Jonas Esq/Hon Sec/Webb Memorial/Fund.

A different type of activity might be included in this collection. This is the medallion for the National Aerial Campaign of 1912. The obverse shows two primitive aircraft: a monoplane with bicycle landing wheels, and a box-kite bi-plane flying against banks of clouds with a church steeple and roof-tops in the background. The reverse reads 1912/National/Aerial/Campaign with the prohetic legend 'Britain's Future is in the Air'.

The World Cup of Association Football produced a striking medallion for Munich in 1974 with the trophy in relief on the reverse side and the legend 'World Cup, FIFA, 1974'.

John Pinches issued an unusual medal in 1971 commemorating the 100th Open Championship that was held at Royal Birkdale. The obverse shows a strong head and shoulders portrait in relief of Willie Park, the winner of the first Open in 1860 that was staged at Prestwick with an entry of eight players. The winning total was 174, the prize a Championship Belt, which was replaced by the present Cup after young Tom Morris had won the Belt outright after three wins in succession. The reverse shows the clubhouse of the Royal and Ancient Golf Club in relief.

Cricket has several attractive medallions. That for the Lord's Centenary as a cricket ground, 1814–1914 is very much a collector's item. To mark County Cricket 1873–1973 the Test and County Cricket Board invited John Pinches to produce a medal that shows on the obverse a scene of a game in progress at Lord's with the famous pavilion in the background. The reverse shows the official badges of all seventeen of the first-class county cricket clubs. The Tower Mint issued a fine medallion showing the pavilion at Lord's in impressive relief with the wording 'Lord's Cricket Ground'; on the reverse is the famous weathervane with Father Time holding the scythe and removing a bail from the wicket. The wording reads: 'England v Australia 1880–1890'. The Test Cricket Centenary 1877–1977 inspired the issue of a silver medal showing a batsman at the wicket with the wicket-keeper with the reverse side carrying the inscription: 'Test Cricket Centenary, Melbourne Cricket Ground, 1877–1977, Australia–England' with crossed bats and ball at the base.

CHAPTER 13

MEMORIES OF SPORTING HISTORY

Collecting postcards has once again caught the imagination, renewed interest being reflected in inflated prices. Cards originally sold for coppers are now changing hands for pounds, even up to three figures. That does not mean bargains cannot be found. The very scale of their original release must mean that, hidden away in attics or junk shops, must lie albums of forgotten cards. The statistics speak for themselves. One publisher at the beginning of the century stated he had issued 43 million postcards in one year with certain popular cards having a circulation of more than a million, whilst in 1905 the Post Office throughout the world handled seven thousand million postcards – a staggering figure that did not include those never posted but put into albums. There is ample scope for every taste with a nostalgic appeal for glimpses of tastes and foibles of a distant past. In that sense postcards are human documents of social history.

The range of sporting events and personalities offer a wealth of variety. Virtually every major sport is documented with the bonus of photographs of the participants. Vague names that appear in record books become real people. Just as interesting are the cards, particularly with golf, that turn back the years and show well-known venues as they once were.

Horseracing cards have many such glimpses. King Edward VII is shown with the royal party in front of the stands at Doncaster for the 1903 St Leger, and again in the Royal Box at Goodwood. This course features prominently in cards of that period, likewise Chester. The setting and grandstands of Newmarket are almost unrecognisable. Occasionally foreign racing cards can be found like the Paddock at Poona where

Henley Regatta.

H. R. H. THE PRINCE OF WALES'S "PERSIMMON". WINNER OF THE DERBY 1896.

crinolined racegoers overshadow the horses; an Edwardian race at Marseilles where camera speeds could not match the horses; and the Derby at Chantilly with fashionably dressed, long-skirted women glancing at the runners. Racehorses and jockeys are numerous. Several exist of Persimmon, Derby winner of 1896 for the Prince of Wales, also Diamond Jubilee, who achieved the unique distinction of winning the Triple Crown for the same owner, who added the Grand National with Ambush II. Among other Derby winners are Jeddah, Caltee More, Volodvovski, Rock Sand and Flying Fox. The statue of Hyperion, winner of the 1933 Derby and the smallest to do so since Little Wonder had won ninety-three years earlier, stands proudly at Newmarket and also figures on a postcard. Similar treatment was accorded to Chamossaire, winner of the 1945 St Leger. Most of the leading jockeys appear on cards, including J.E. Watts who won the 1927 Derby on Call Boy; Danny Maher who collected nine Classic wins including the Derby on Rock Sand (1903), Cicero (1905) and Spearmint (1906); George Archibald, American jockey, winner of the 1922 Two Thousand Guineas on St Louis; Sam Loates, with seven Classic successes including the 1895 Derby on Sir Visto and the dead-heat on Harvester (1884); another old-timer is Otto Madden, Hungarian jockey, winner of the 1898 Derby on Jeddah; more modern jockeys include Steve Donoghue, Gordon Richards, Scobie Breasley, and Lester Piggott.

The Boat Race has a long sequence of cards showing both race and crews from the end of last century. Henley, particularly the Edwardian period, is well represented with the emphasis on the fashionable side as opposed to the serious business of rowing. Baseball features such stars as 'Babe' Ruth and Lou Gehrig of the 'Yankees', Karl Hubbell of the 'Giants', Max Bishop of 'Athletics', and Dazzy Vance of 'Robins'. Douglas Clark is styled the world's champion wrestler Cumberland and Westmoreland style. C.B. Kingsbury, Olympic cycling champion of 1908, is also recorded on a postcard as are Captain Matthew Webb and T.W. Burgess, two of the earliest Channel swimmers. Tossing the Caber at the Highland Games is also featured. George Hackenschmidt is depicted showing the world championship belt as well as his over-developed

(*opposite above*): Even last century the Thames became a leisured river carnival during Henley week. (*below*): Persimmon, the bay, bred and owned by the Prince of Wales, after winning the 1898 Derby.

muscles and several demonstrating wrestling holds. Tom Burrows is featured as champion club swinger.

Lawn Tennis has a comprehensive gallery of the world's leading players from the beginning of the century, including early scenes at Queen's Club and Wimbledon.

Association Football concentrates on team photographs in which many famous old players appear. Occasionally there are studies of individuals like Patsy Gallacher, Stanley Matthews and C.B. Fry listed as Southampton and Corinthian. Rugby Football also contents itself with groups, particularly the New Zealand, South African and Australian touring sides over many years.

Motor-racing, as opposed to motoring, has a limited number of cards though a crowd scene at the Speedway in New York early this century looks somewhat incongruous with top-hatted spectators accompanied by women dressed as for Goodwood lining the track without any protection. Early drivers featured include Louis Chiron, Fagioli, Count Trossi, the Hon. Brian Lewis and George Eyston.

Boxing has a substantial number of cards issued over a period of years and many weights though emphasis is laid on the heavyweight class. The champions featured include Joe Louis, Jake Kilrain, John L. Sullivan, John Knifton, Peter Jackson, Jim Mace, Joe Beckett, Georges Carpentier, Johnny Summers, Johnny Best, Sam Langford, Johnny Dundee, Jack Johnson, Tommy Farr, Nel Tarleton, Randolph Turpin, Gene Tunney, Jack Dempsey, Max Baer, Cassius Clay and Larry Holmes.

Golf has a valuable selection of early postcards. Scenes of the Old Course at St Andrews in the last century are interesting. Those of the Edwardian period show many famous old players, men like J.E. Laidlay, Mure Fergusson, John Ball, Harold Hilton and Freddie Tait. The Triumvirate of J.H. Taylor, James Braid and Harry Vardon are engaged in matches as young men. Sandy Herd is shown with his distinctive finish to a full drive. Other featured personalities include A.J. Balfour, the Earl of Dudley, the Hon. A. Lyttelton, Lord Balfour of Burleigh, Jack White, George Duncan and many others. North Berwick was extremely popular at the beginning of the century and many cards show what it was like

(*opposite above*): The tranquil peace of Queen's Club at the beginning of this century in striking contrast to (*below*) Sir Malcolm Campbell's record of 301 mph in Bluebird.

"Bluebird" hurtling over the measured mile.
From a sketch by Bryan de Grineau of "The Motor"

Johnny Best. Scottish Fly-weight Champion.

Johnny Best, fighter turned promoter who helped Tarleton, Roderick and Kane to world title bouts.

with golfers playing in the then traditional red coats. Others featured include Nairn, with its primitive clubhouse; Rye, Carnoustie in the very early days; Cruden Bay; Westward Ho with the old golf pavilion; Sunningdale, Prestwick, Sandwich, Hunstanton and Hoylake. In lighter vein several theatrical ladies were featured either clutching a pencil-shaped golf bag with hickory clubs or else at the completion of what

The terrace of the Royal and Ancient Clubhouse at St Andrews with the Waters of
Eden in the background.

was intended to be a golf shot. A pretty young Gladys Cooper with
wide-brimmed hat is shown at the end of a sweeping drive, but instead
of looking at what had happened to the shot, her eyes are turned to see
where the camera is sited. At least a bunker in the background adds an
authentic touch. Very often these photographs came in sets of six with
hand-tinted effects. By reversing the negatives and giving the clothes a
different colour, it was necessary for only three photographs to be ac-
tually taken.

Cricket has an overwhelming flood of postcards. Virtually every player
of note since the heyday of W.G. Grace was featured, either singly or in
county or national groups. A comprehensive collection could be a visual
history of the game's personalities. Cricket grounds are featured including one showing the Australians leaving the pavilion at the Crystal
Palace ground on the occasion of their first match, 4 May 1905, led by
their captain, Joseph Darling, who between 1894 and 1905 made
thirty-four Test appearances. Another series shows some of the treasures

Lord Hawke, one of the great personalities of cricket at every level.

of Lord's including the urn containing the ashes of a ball, with its embroidered velvet bag, being presented to the Hon Ivo Bligh, captain of the English team in Australia 1882–3, to mark their victory by two matches to one against W.L. Murdoch's team. This followed the mock obituary notice that appeared in the *Sporting Times*:

> 'In affectionate remembrance of
> English Cricket which died on
> The Oval, on August 29th 1882.
> Deeply lamented by a large circle
> of sorrowing friends and acquaint–
> ances. R.I.P. The body will be
> cremated and the Ashes taken to
> Australia.'

The events that prompted this gesture came after England, faced with 85 to win, began their second innings at 3.45 pm on the second day. Boyle and Spofforth wrought havoc. Seven wickets fell for 70. Still with 3 wickets to fall and 15 runs needed, victory looked likely. Those last 3 wickets went with only 7 added to the total and that included 3 byes. Victory went to Australia by 7 runs. On his death in 1927, Ivo Bligh, then Lord Darnley, bequested the Ashes to the MCC in his will. The urn containing the Ashes is now in the Imperial Cricket Memorial Museum.

CHAPTER 14

THE WORLD OF GOLF

The memorabilia of golf includes a range of items so varied that classification is difficult. The easiest way is to describe in detail part of a collection.

A blue and white early nineteenth-century Delft dish with a centre-piece showing a Dutch scene with golfers playing on the ice is similar to the designs on early Delft tiles. Among the golfers Sir Leslie Ward featured in his Spy caricatures were J.H. Taylor, Horace Hutchinson and John Ball Jnr. Among several Royal Doulton pieces is a stoneware vase, impressed Doulton, Lambeth England 165, with raised white motifs of golfers on both sides; this item frequently comes up for sale at London auctions. Rarer is a Royal Doulton punch bowl with a cream base and coloured transfers of golfers in Jacobean dress both inside and outside.

A Bilston enamel box shows on the outside the first green of the Old Course at St Andrews in 1798, with the clubhouse of the Royal and Ancient in the background. Another pleasing oval box has a rural setting with winding river, the principal subject being an Edwardian lady golfer with long flowing skirt, tight jacket and fashionable hat. The artist has frozen the club at the top of the backswing that is so full that in no way could she have struck the ball from such a pose, as the male onlooker must have known.

An interesting photograph of a tournament played at Leith Links on 17 May 1867 shows a group of Bob Kirk, James Anderson, Andrew Strath, Tom Morris, Andrew Greig, Willie Dunn, George Morris, Willie Dow and Tom Morris Jnr. Examples such as these are valuable visual historical reminders of the past and are frequently offered for sale. They bring the shadowy figures of the past to life and provide details of dress and equipment as well as background. Of great rarity is a different type of photograph, the golfing daguerreotype. To understand how this type of picture came into being it is necessary to hie back to 1837, the year when Queen Victoria came to the throne and Louis Daguerre produced the first successful dageurreotype. The method was revolutionary. He sensitised in iodine vapour a polished copper plate coated with silver, exposed it in the camera, developed it with mercury vapour, and fixed the resulting image with a common salt solution. Sir John Herschel, the astronomer, became interested in this new phenomenon, and suggested the use of 'hypo' (sodium theosulphate) instead of salt for fixing the image. The idea worked and was soon adopted, but there was one disadvantage. Because the first daguerreotypes were on a solid metal plate, it was almost impossible to make additional copies and because of the very long exposure time needed (between fifteen and twenty minutes) only static scenes without movement of any kind could be recorded.

Louis Daguerre (1787–1851), who gave his name to the daguerreotype, is without doubt the best known of the photographic inventors. He started his working life as a scene painter in Paris theatres and as an artist. Becoming interested in photography, he published an account of his process which ran into thirty editions in two years. He was showered with honours including the *Pour le Merité* from Prussia and a life pension by the French Government. Any daguerreotype is rare. In the example described above both golfer and young caddie must have been motionless for a long time as the long-nosed club is clear in line, likewise details of the clothes.

Golfing figures are rare. Staffordshire potters produced a Victorian pair of Scottish golfers in the fashions of that time, not objects of beauty but interesting. More realistic is a lifelike bronze of J.H. Taylor, recognisable by the stance, cap and aggressive projecting jaw. Three miniature figures of an even earlier period are delightful: the woman wears a long, full skirt, long tight jacket and the inevitable hat; the man, in long stockings, breeches and jacket, looks every inch a golfer; whilst the caddie clutching the clubs is accurate in every detail. Miscellaneous items include a fob watch in the form of a gutty ball; various commemorative mugs of Open Championships with Birkdale, giving a lay-out of the course; a toast rack with fourteen clubs leaning towards each other and golf balls at either end; Louis Wain lithographs showing cats playing golf; a walking stick in form of a stylised bulger driver with an ivory sole. Goss produced several light-hearted golfing pieces; pot-lids;

Victorian match-box holders with Victorian golfers on the sides; modern paperweights with the top quarter cut away to show golfers in silhouette.

Lastly and most important the collector of golf memorabilia should concentrate on antique golf clubs, golf balls and golfing books. The appeal has caught on as the sales held by Christie's and Sotheby's have shown, but bargains are still to be found provided you can spot the pitfalls. With prices rising the field is wide open for forgeries. Hugh Philp clubs come up for auction from time to time and fetch very high prices. Occasionally one appears made of persimmon. That in itself proves it was a fake for this particular wood only appeared in this country from America some fifty years after Philp's death. This craftsman only made clubs of apple, thorn and pear, particularly the last-named. Generally speaking the old wood-shafted clubs offer a wide range. A rut iron by John Gray, dated about 1850, was picked up in a junk shop for a couple of pounds. Some of the old clubs to look for include the long-nosed putters by Robert Forgan; any club stamped T. Morris, particularly the bulbous-headed putters; McEwans beautiful wooden clubs; J.H. Taylor's wooden putters. Other famous names include Auchterlonie, Willie Park, J. Anderson, Willie Dunn and Harry Vardon. Occasionally a Schenectady aluminium putter can be found; William Hunter produced bulger drivers; whilst clubs by Ben Sayers, Walter Hagen and Henry Cotton are collectable. Baffing spoons, wry-necked iron putters, smooth-faced irons, brass-soled wooden niblicks, jiggers, early cleeks and mallet-headed putters make up but a fraction of the old clubs that must be stored away in dusty corners. Freak clubs can also be found. Four gathered into one lot at a Sotheby sale were a wooden brass-soled croquet-type three-sided putter, a T-shaped putter, an aluminium circular putter and a hammer-shaped club.

Equally desirable and just as rare are old golf balls. Anyone who owns a feather golf ball has a valuable property. Two such balls stamped T. Morris and dated about 1840 were sold by Sotheby's for £1,400, whilst another by Wm Gourlay fetched £1,600. Such inflated prices are prompted, as so often happens, by two keen bidders both anxious to buy at any cost. So much depends on the condition of the balls and who were the makers. The same applies to gutta-percha balls with the bramble pattern produced from a mould. Occasionally it is possible to find cast-iron golf ball moulds with the raised mesh design in two parts. As

Superb bronze figure of J.H. Taylor, five times Open champion.

Freddie Tait lines-up a putt on the first green against John Ball, who won the
Amateur Championship eight times.

with old clubs, the range is considerable, including the smooth gutty of
about 1848; the Silvertown 'Snipit' hand-hammered red gutta; the
Thornton hand-hammered ball of 1880; the Willie Park Junr 'Royal' of
1896; the 'Sturrock' canvas-covered; the Henry's Rilfed of 1902; the
'Eclipse' of 1870; the machine-marked 'Eclipse' of ten years later; the
hand-hammered and moulded ball by Cockburn of Edinburgh, about
1885; the Inglis 'Unique' of 1902; and the Haskins of Hoylake ball of
about 1897. There many other makes, sufficient to make an interesting
and valuable collection illustrating golf ball development that takes up
little space.

As regards golf books there is scope for building up a good library of
literature on the sport provided it is selective. Quantity is no substitute
for rarity. H.S. Everad wrote in 1896 that he had 'serious misgiving as
to the propriety of inflicting another book on golfers already satiated
with the literature on the subject'. If he felt like that when the first
American book on golf had just been published, heaven knows what

his reaction would have been today to the flood of golf books from professionals who have to hire journalistic hacks to string their words and theories together. As a guide, I list here fifty books that reflect various aspects and periods of the game.

Take a rare book first: *The Golfers Manual* (1857) by H.B. Farnie ranks as the first text-book on the game. Originally written under the nom-de-plume of 'a keen hand' with the secondary sub-title 'an historical and descriptive account of the national game of Scotland', it was re-printed in London by the Dropmore Press in 1947.

Any list of outstanding twentieth-century prose writers must include Bernard Darwin. His first article appeared in *The Times* in 1907 and he continued to write regularly for that newspaper for the next forty-six years, as well as contributing to *Country Life*. His style changed sports writing into a form of literary journalism. His pen, rich in charm and fluency, produced more than twenty books. In making my choice a little cheating is permissible. Counting as one, it is the autobiographical trilogy: *Green Memories* (1928), *Life is sweet, brother* (1940), and *The world that Fred made* (1955).

My third choice would be an anthology, *Around golf* (1939) edited by J.S.F. Morrison with such contributors as Joyce Wethered, Guy Campbell, Bernard Darwin, A.P.F. Chapman, Ben Travers, Henry Longhurst and Cyril Tolley.

Robert Clark's *Golf: a royal and ancient game* was published in 1875. The author was an Edinburgh printer who, with tireless patience, gathered historical data of immense interest, plus extracts from the Minute books of the earliest golf clubs together with biographical sketches. A second edition appeared in 1893. Facsimile reprints were produced in Britain in 1975 and the United States of America in 1976.

Entirely different is *This life I've led* by Mildred 'Babe' Zaharias. Published in 1956, it tells the remarkable story of this outstanding golfer and athlete who is claimed to have broken the world record the first time she threw the javelin. In the 1932 Olympic Games she won Gold Medals for the javelin and the 80-metres hurdles and a Silver Medal for the high jump. As a woman golfer she was in a class of her own. The year the book was published her terminal illness of cancer was diagnosed. It is a story of great interest.

H.S.C. Everard's book *A history of the Royal and Ancient Golf Club, St Andrews, 1754–1900*, published in 1907, is a well-documented histor-

Characteristic finish of Arthur James Balfour, Captain of the Royal and Ancient Club in 1894.

ical volume in considerable detail, while for those interested in the theoretical approach to the game P.A. Vaile wrote an instructional manual *The Short Game*, published in Chicago 1929, with an English edition in 1936 and an introduction by Henry Longhurst. Another historical book of rarity and a useful sourcebook is John Kerr's *Golf book of East Lothian* published in 1896. Entirely different is Patric Dickenson's *A round of golf courses: a selection of the best eighteen*, published in 1951. An antique item is Robert Forgan's *Golfer's Handbook* (1881). It is a mine of information about the history of the game, with instructional tips, details of leading clubs and office bearers assembled in a slim book by the founder of the St Andrews club-making firm. The saga of Bobby Jones's famous 'grand slam' season is recorded in the well-documented book *Down the Fairway* by the combined efforts of Jones and Oscar Keeler. The first edition appeared in 1927. Two autobiographical books I regard as a single volume. They come from the pen of the versatile Henry Longhurst – *It was Good while it Lasted* (1941) and *My Life and Soft Times* (1971). Together they form a fascinating pen portrait of a golf writer who must rank second to Bernard Darwin for apt phrases and lingering descriptions. Unlike todays television commentators, he did not try to sell himself on the screen, but let the picture tell its own story with pertinent comments. He applied the same technique to the written word.

Equally entertaining in a different century is Sir Walter Simpson's *The Art of Golf* (1887) packed with choice observations and the first to use instructional photographs. This former captain of the Honourable Company of Edinburgh Golfers would have dipped his pen in acid today had he to comment on the current scene. Several books came from the pen of Horace G. Hutchinson, the first Englishman to become captain of the Royal and Ancient Club. *Golf* in the Badminton Library of Sports became a best-seller, but preference goes to *Fifty Years of Golf* published in 1919. An unusual book by Ford Frick is *This is St Andrews* (1973), a history of America's oldest golf club. Another excellent club history was written by Guy B. Farrar, keen ornithologist and one-time secretary of the Royal Liverpool at Hoylake. In 1933 he wrote *The Royal Liverpool Golf Club: a history, 1869–1932*. He gives in great detail the early history and details of the personalities of the St Andrews of England. *Famous Fairways* (1968) is another well-written book by Sir Peter Allen that concentrates on British and overseas championship courses. George C. Nash struck fresh ground with *Letters to the Secretary of a Golf Club* (1935). The possibilities of such a theme are endless and Nash did not miss a trick. Another anthology edited by Peter Lawless reflects his painstaking approach to the game. His death during the war was a great loss. *The Golfer's Companion* (1937) included contributions from Robert H.K. Browning, Alfred Padgham, Henry Cotton, Eleanor Helme, Bernard Darwin, Hylton Cleaver, R.C. Robertson-Glasgow and O.B. Keeler. Roger Wethered and Tom Simpson produced the classic work on golf course architecture and golf course construction in *The Architectural Side of Golf* (1929). Simpson was a rare character with set views and grim determination to justify what were sometimes controversial theories. Even if you disagree, the chapters make agreeable reading. An interesting biography, *My Partner, Ben Hogan* (1954), came from that highly individualistic and colourful professional, Jimmy Demaret, who died in 1983. To many people, Ben Hogan stands out as America's greatest professional with a record to match such a claim. A giant of another century was further immortalised by Willie Tulloch in 1907 with *Life of Tom Morris: with glimpses of St Andrews and its golfing celebrities*. This is a collector's gem.

Golfing Curios and the Like (1910) by Harry B. Wood is a mine of information on early equipment with chapters on the history of the game. Highly rated among collectors, it was reprinted in facsimile in 1980 by Pride Publications of Manchester. *The Story of American Golf* (1948) by Herbert Warren Wind is very readable. A third edition published in 1975 brings it more up-to-date with doubtless a fourth edition in the offing. An unusual book and difficult to find is *Originaes Golfianae* edited by Arthur Taylor with the somewhat wordy subtitle *The birth of golf and its early childhood as revealed in a chance-discovered manuscript from a Scottish monastery*. Stephen Potter introduces a new dimension in *Complete Golf Gamesmanship* (1968), an invaluable manual for those who wish to win by skirting the boundaries of cheating. Francis Ouimet, the first American to become captain of the Royal and Ancient, wrote his reminiscences in *A Game of Golf* (1932). Gary Player added his thoughts with *Grand Slam Golf* (1966) that explains something of his tenacious driving-force. Andrew Lang takes us back to a more tranquil period in *A Batch of Golfing Papers* (1892) edited by R. Barclay that includes an entertaining chapter describing Doctor Johnson's reaction to golf at St Andrews during his Scottish tour. P.G. Wodehouse took such experiences a stage further in *Heart of a Goof* (1926).

James Balfour adds an authentic touch to descriptions of the game on the Old Course in the last century in *Reminiscences of Golf on St Andrews Links* (1887). For those anxious to improve their shotmaking, Tommy Armour produced a first-class book in *How to Play Your Best Golf all the Time* (1954). The title alone was a bait. If you wish to delve deeper, Haultain's *The Mystery of Golf* (1908) will unravel the mental hazards of swinging a club; at least that was the intention though conceivably it might convert you to hockey. *The Greatest Game of All* (1969) by Jack Nicklaus will restore the balance. Joyce Wethered's *Golfing Memories and Methods* (1933) should be in every collection, likewise Andrew Kirkaldy's *Fifty Years of Golf: My Memories* (1921), and Henry Cotton's *Thanks for the Game* (1980). An interesting early instructional manual is *Our Lady of the Green* by Louie MacKern and M. Boys (1899). The first professional book along the same lines was by Willie Park Jr, *The Game of Golf* (1896) which includes a section on the art of greenkeeping. An unusual golf book by Frederick George Mann, *Lord Rutherford and the Golf Course* (1976), describes how the nuclear scientist, Lord Rutherford, was attracted to the game.

Eleanor E. Helme pursued a lighter vein in her autobiography *After the Ball* (1931) with the subtitle *Merry memoirs of a golfer, being the story of 46 championships and other golfing occasions pursued with club, notebook and pencil.* More down to earth is *Unplayable Lies* (1965) by that tough character Fred Corcoran. May Hezlet produced a book that today has historical value, *Ladies Golf* (1904). Left-handed golfers who sometimes feel they are disregarded in the way of equipment and instruction can take heart from Bob Charles's *The Left-Hander from New Zealand* (1965). Enid Wilson's *A Gallery of Women Golfers* (1961) contains innumerable vignettes from the pen of one of the greatest women golfers. *The World of Golf* (1963) by Charles Price is a well-written, authoritative volume. *Scotland's Gift – Golf* (1928) reflects the experience of the American golf course architect, Charles B. MacDonald. *The Glorious World of Golf* (1973) by Peter Dobereiner is a handsome production delightfully written. *Curious History of the Golf Ball* (1968) is an authoritative work by J.S. Martin. Finally *The Birdie Book: a miscellany of golf* edited by Robert Rodrigo in 1967 must surely be the ideal bedside book with such a team of outstanding writers.

Given in list form below, these choices but touch the fringe of what can be found, but it would form the nucleus of a golfing library.

 1... *The Golfer's Manual* by H.B. Farnie
 2... *Green Memories*
     Life is sweet, brother   triology by Bernard Darwin
     The world that Fred made
 3... *Around golf* edited by J.S.F. Morrison
 4... *Golf a royal and ancient game* by Robert Clark
 5... *This life I've led* by Mildred Zaharias
 6... *A history of the Royal and Ancient Golf Club, St Andrews 1754–1900* by H.S.C. Everard
 7... *The Short Game* by P.A. Vaile
 8... *Golf Book of East Lothian* by John Kerr
 9... *A round of golf courses* by Patric Dickenson
10... *Golfer's Handbook* by Robert Forgan
11... *Down the Fairway* by Bobby Jones and Oscar Keeler
12... *It was Good while it lasted*
     My Life and Soft Times by Henry Longhurst
13... *The Art of Golf* by Sir Walter Simpson
14... *Fifty Years of Golf* by Horace G. Hutchinson
15... *This is St Andrews* by Ford Frick
16... *The Royal Liverpool Golf Club* by Guy B. Farrar
17... *Famous Fairways* by Sir Peter Allen
18... *Letters to the Secretary of a Golf Club* by George C. Nash
19... *The Golfer's Companion* edited by Peter Lawless
20... *The Architectural Side of Golf* by Roger Wethered and Tom Campbell
21... *My Partner, Ben Hogan* by Jimmy Demaret
22... *Life of Tom Morris* by Willie Tulloch
23... *Golfing Curios and the Like* by Harry B. Wood
24... *The Story of American Golf* by Herbert Warren Wind
25... *Originaes Golfianae* edited by Arthur Taylor
26... *Complete Golf Gamesmanship* by Stephen Potter
27... *A Game of Golf* by Francis Ouimet
28... *Grand Slam Golf* by Gary Player
29... *A Batch of Golfing Papers* edited by R. Barclay
30... *Heart of a Goof* by P.G. Wodehouse

31... *Reminiscences of Golf on St Andrews Links* by James Balfour

32... *How to Play Your Best Golf all the Time* by Tommy Armour

33... *The Mystery of Golf* by T.A. Haultain

34... *The Greatest Game of All* by Jack Nicklaus

35... *Golfing Memories and Methods* by Joyce Wethered

36... *Fifty Years of Golf* by Andrew Kirkaldy

37... *Thanks for the Game* by Henry Cotton

38... *Our Lady of the Green* by Louie MacKern and M. Boys

39... *The Game of Golf* by Willie Park Jr.

40... *Lord Rutherford and the Golf Course* by Frederick George Mann

41... *After the Ball* by Eleanor E. Helme

42... *Unplayable Lies* by Fred Corcoran

43... *Ladies' Golf* by May Hezlet

44... *The Left Hander from New Zealand* by Bob Charles

45... *A Gallery of Women Golfers* by Enid Wilson

46... *The World of Golf* by Charles Price

47... *Scotland's Gift – Golf* by Charles B. MacDonald

48... *The Glorious World of Golf* by Peter Dobereiner

49... *Curious History of the Golf Ball* by J.S. Martin

50... *The Birdie Book* edited by Robert Rodrigo

For the benefit of those who are not particularly interested in golf books, here are six suggestions to add to the memorabilia collection. Rare and choice is a six-inch Royal Worcester mug bearing the famous painting by L.F. Abbott of the Blackheath Golfers, depicting the golfer and his caddie; date about 1790, when the artist completed the work. The Burslem potter, MacIntyre, produced a dish bearing the outline of the ace of clubs with a centre-piece of a golfer at the top of his swing. It would hardly win a prize as an object of beauty, but it is unusual. Some of the old postcards depict most of the early golfers like John Ball, Tom Morris, Harold Hilton, Lord Balfour, and J.E. Laidlay, whilst early postcards show the old club-houses of many well-known clubs as well as glimpses of links when course maintenance was helped by sheep. Music

Stylish study of Gladys Cooper, hopefully suggestive that she had played a shot.

sheets are not plentiful. One of the most popular was the *Gleneagles foxtrot*. Postage stamps can now constitute a gallery of golf champions as well as First Day Covers to mark the Open Championship. The final suggestion is a Spy cartoon that I have tried in vain for many years to find. It depicts Hoylake Golf Course and originally appeared in the *Vanity Fair* issue of 16 July 1903.

CHAPTER 15

COLLECTING CRICKET BATS

Collecting cricket bats has a two-fold interest: age and association. Rarities are the primitive examples that reflect the evolutionary processes that shaped the game. Some time ago a fine example of a mid-eighteenth-century bat came on the market. It was of curved shape and made for a left-hander by T. Johnson of Southfleet, Kent. Without a background knowledge of eighteenth-century cricket, its significance and purpose would be missed. To all intents and purposes it could have been a cumbersome weapon, instead of a very rare find.

In the early days of the Hambledon Club, about 1755, bowling was under-arm and along the ground. Bats were curved to deal with this type of delivery, the weight being at the end like a hockey stick. The stroke was a slashing affair as early prints show, and the odds were in favour of accurate bowling. A perfect example can be seen in the pavilion at the Oval. It is thought to be the oldest known bat and belonged to John Chitty in 1729, weighs 2 lb 4 oz, and is shaped like a hockey stick.

The change came when John Small the elder, of Petersfield, a cobbler by trade, introduced the first straight bat with shoulders in 1773. He found that an upright bat made defence of the wicket much easier and demonstrated the fact in a match between Hambledon and England when his innings lasted for three days. His batting technique was to get the front foot across the wicket with the bat turned slightly back, relying on wrist action. It was so effective it was not often that anyone bowled him out. This revolutionary idea caused a change in bowling technique. Under-arm hugging the ground made way for the pitched-up bowling

Early bats are the pride of any cricketing collection, but are exceptionally rare.

143

The condition of cricket in 1744 produced curved bats, underarm bowling and two stumps.

of Tom Walker and David Harris. Such was the success of Small's bat that in 1775 he gave up cobbling and set himself up as a batmaker. The bat was made in one piece.

The year 1845 saw the next change with the introduction of whalebone handles. Eight years later came the significant improvement of the cane handle. There were occasional variations from other theorists. Thomas White of Reigate produced a bat in a game between Hambledon and Chertsey on 23 September 1771 that was wider than the wickets. The reaction of authority was prompt. The minutes of a Hambledon Club meeting on 25 September read:

'In view of the performance of one White at Rye-
gate on September 23rd that four and quarter
inches shall be the breadth of bats forthwith.
                                    Richard Nyren
                                    T. Brett
                                    J. Small.'

To make sure the law was enforced an iron frame was made for the
Hambledon Club and kept as a bat-gauge to check any doubtful blade.
In 1835 the length of the bat was limited to 38 inches including the
handle.

Any bats from this period are rare, but collectors find interest in
autographed bats that are comparatively common. Among those sold
at very reasonable prices are bats signed by the England and Australian
teams of 1938, 1934, 1930, West Indies of 1933, and individual signatures on personal bats belonging to Peter May, Rohan Kanhai, Percy
Fender, Len Hutton and Jack Hobbs. Only seldom does a W.G. Grace
bat appear and, of course, fetches a good price. Easier to display are the
miniature bats bearing Test Match signatures.

CHAPTER 16

A SPECIALISED SPORT

Coursing is a specialised sport that attracts as many detractors as supporters. It is a reflection of days when sporting activities were more robust and less sensitive. The rules by which coursing is governed were drawn up at the instigation of Queen Elizabeth I. Thomas, Duke of Norfolk, was ordered to prepare 'laws of the leash and coursing'. The mounted, red-coated judge has to consider the points of the course, virtually taken from the Elizabethan rules. They are six in number and include *speed*, the *go-by*, the *turn*, the *wench*, the *kill* and the *trip*. It does not necessarily follow that the greyhound which kills the hare wins the course. The dog that best conforms to these points is the winner and often the poorer dog makes the kill.

The rules were first tested at Wortley Park in Gloucestershire when Queen Elizabeth I and Lord Leicester coursed in Lord Berkeley's park. It was here that Shakespeare coursed his greyhound 'Lady' and in all his plays he uses the correct coursing terms. The Queen unquestionably approved of 'two staunch greyhounds standing in the slips'. For centuries the greyhound has been the favourite of royalty, the symbol of a gentleman of blood and coat-armour, as when the historian Froissart rode to the Border Wars on a grey horse with falcon on wrist and white greyhound running alongside.

The peak of the coursing world is the Waterloo Cup at Altcar, the equivalent to the Derby and the Grand National on the Turf. Inaugurated in 1836, it has continued to hold its premier place and it is from this event that collector's items can be found. Two greyhounds have been singled out for special treatment as a result of their records. One is Pretender, a light brown greyhound of whom there is a Staffordshire pottery figure, ten inches high, made in 1871. The companion figure is the legendary Master McGrath, the black greyhound belonging

Lord Lurgan's black greyhound, Master M'Grath, won the blue ribbon of the coursing world in 1868–9 and beat Pretender in 1871.

to Lord Lurgan, who won the blue riband of the coursing world, the Waterloo Cup, in 1868, 1869 and 1871 (beating Pretender), a feat that ranked him, according to some experts, as the most remarkable greyhound ever put into the slips. The issue of *The Illustrated London News* for 11 March 1871 reported that 'his speed was terrific and his cleverness and killing powers equal to it; indeed, he never gave any of his opponents a chance'. Lord Lurgan received a command from the Queen to take the greyhound to Windsor for her inspection. He became, as a writer in *Country Life* of 9 February 1956, declared 'the most famous dog that ever lived. His name was known in the humblest cottage, his deeds were celebrated in song and ballad, his picture was to be seen everywhere'. The fulsome words went somewhat over the top and admirers of Mick the Miller may have other views, but there is no doubt that Master McGrath was a celebrity, and it was true that his success was celebrated in song.

The sentiment matched the mood of Victorian England, an age of live entertainment from musical soirées to exuberant performances in music halls and taverns. There was a demand for sheet music of every description, for bawdy songs and sentimental ballads, subject-matter ranging from the topical to the tragic, from the romantic to the ridiculous. The decorative covers of the sheets reflected the life of that period. Occasionally the taste was doubtful but the craftsmanship was often superb. Among them *The Coursers Galop* paid a tribute to Master McGrath. It is 'most Respectfully Dedicated to the Above Noblemen and Gentlemen', referring to fourteen coloured cameo likenesses of Mr J. Hedley, the Judge; Mr J. Bell, Flag Steward; T. Briggs, esq.; E.W. Stocker, esq.; Samuel Mallaby, esq.; Jamie Bake, esq.; J. Legn, MP; Colonel Goodlake, VC; Earl of Stair; Earl of Haddington; Earl of Sefton; and Lord Lurgan. The centre of the music-sheet shows Bab-at-the-Bowster and Master McGrath held by Tom Raper, with the red-coated Judge on horseback, and top-hatted spectators in the background. At the foot of the sheet the composer, Ernest J. Macdonald, inserted his own picture. Staffordshire potters issued a ten-inch model of the dog with the name in raised capitals, whilst a tasteful and elegant painting of Master McGrath by J.E. Dean on enamel is a worthy addition to any collection.

CHAPTER 17

THE ATTRACTIONS OF CARTOPHILY

It is just over a century ago that cigarette cards first appeared. Since then more than 15,000 different subjects have been produced, catering in serious but entertaining vein for every conceivable taste. Narrowing the range to sporting topics offers the collector a panorama of sporting personalities, household names whom we see again in their prime. Memories never age. Cartophily is widening its appeal accompanied by the inevitable increase in prices, sometimes into three figures, but bargains are still to be found. In this chapter it is possible only to comment on a cross-section, but those chosen are issues of merit. The racing scene, although not as numerous as other sports, nevertheless has at least ten sets that should be sought. In 1923 two excellent series were issued by W. Sandorides of London; 50 *Famous Racehorses* and 50 *Famous Racecourses*. Neither are common. The same can be said of *Owners and Jockeys*, a set of 20 produced by Salmon and Gluckstein in 1900. Players issued a popular series in 1933 of 50 *Derby and Grand National Winners* in which we see such famous horses as Minoru, Spion Kop, Manna, April the Fifth, Grakle, Call Boy, Sprig and Sergeant Murphy with their jockeys up and owners' colours. Carrolls of Dublin produced a set of 25 un-numbered cards of historic interest, *Derby Winners*, showing in black and white such horses as Sainfoin (1890), Persimmon (1896) and Flying Fox (1899).

Players *Racing Caricatures* are first class. That of Harry Wragg is a perfect likeness. The same can be said of Tommy Weston who won the Derby on Sansovino and Hyperion. There is the ebullient Charles Smirke who was never troubled by nerves on the big occasion. His Derby wins were with Windsor Lad, Mahmoud, Tulyar and Hard Ridden. Other of his successes included the 2000 Guineas on My Babu and Palestine, the 1000 Guineas on Rose Royale II, and the St Leger with Windsor Lad,

Wills produced this first-class issue of Cricketers in 1928 that contained excellent action studies.

Babram, Tulyar and Never Say Die. His technical ability was impeccable.

Also in the set are the caricatures of Steve Donoghue, the natural successor to Fred Archer; Charles Elliott, the natural jockey who made winning look easy; Bernard Carslake, or 'Brownie' as he was popularly known, who had a long list of successes in spite of weight problems; Joe Childs, an angular character with dark bushy eyebrows, noted for his 'waiting' tactics that brought many Classic wins including the Triple Crown on Gainsborough; while jockeys who won the Grand National include John Anthony on Glenside, the only horse to complete the course without mishap, also Ally Sloper and Troytown: Robert Trudgill on Master Robert; and Freddie Rees on Shaun Spadah. There is Herbert Jones, known to history as the jockey who won the Triple Crown for the Prince of Wales (later King Edward VII) on Diamond Jubilee. Other easily recognisable jockeys include Fred Fox, George Hulme, Edwin Piper, Albert Whalley and Victor Smyth. Historically the set is first class.

Even more so is the issue by Gallahers of *Famous Jockeys* of 1936. Many experts consider it as one of the finest ever issued. All the great jockeys of the 1930s are shown, familiar names like Eph Smith; Fred Lane, who won the 1932 Derby for the actor, Tom Walls, on April the Fifth; Willie Nevett, known as 'The Cock of the North' and three times Derby winner on Owen Tudor, Ocean Swell, and Dante; Gerry Wilson, for ever linked with the record-breaking 'chaser, Golden Miller owned by Miss Dorothy Paget; Charlie Smirke who, as first jockey to the Aga Khan, won the 1936 Derby on Mahmoud, with later wins in this Classic on Tulyar and Hard Ridden as well as Windsor Lad in 1934; Freddy Fox, who was robbed of the Triple Crown on Bahram through a fall in a selling race the day before the St Leger; Bobbie Jones, who mixed his skills – apart from being a brilliant rider he was also a first-class golfer; Joe Marshall, who was equally at home on the flat and over the hurdles, his greatest success coming on Trigo in the 1929 Derby; Dick Perryman, who just failed to beat Coronach in the Derby but made amends by training Airborne to win in 1946; Joe Childs, who not only took the Triple Crown in 1918 on Gainsborough, but won the Derby and the St Leger in 1926 on Coronach, as well as gaining several other Classic wins, plus four successes in the Gold Cup ... Every card is a characteristic glimpse of the jockey with the owner's colours clear and incisive.

R. and J. Lea of Stockport issued a series of 48 cards on *Famous Horses* in 1926 but they are inferior to the Sandorides set. Ogden's had two series of 25 cards giving *Trainers and Owners' Colours*. The idea was good. Photography was used for the trainer's portraits and in that sense the record was accurate. The silks were faithful, but somehow the pairing is not happy. Wills had an imaginative set of 40 large cards,

Racehorses and Jockeys. The year was 1938 and whilst there is a certain amount of repetition with other issues, it is good to see again such horses as Kellsboro' Jack, Battleship and Royal Danieli. Possibly the most colourful set was issued by Gallaher in 1938 and titled *Racing Scenes*. It is just that. Every aspect of the background is covered. There is Steve Donoghue on Brown Jack; the Aga Khan leading in Mahmoud after winning the Derby for the third time; the legendary Golden Miller; Gordon Richards in his prime; Rass Prince Monolulu, the Prince of Tipsters; tic-tac men in action; Captain Allison, the official starter of the Jockey Club; a jockey weighing out: Frank Butters, the Newmarket trainer; Lord Astor and Lord Derby; Sir Humphrey de Trafford and Joe Lawson; Freddie Fox on Bahram; R.C. Lyle broadcasting a race in front of primitive equipment; Becher's Brook and Tattenham Corner; breaking in a yearling; a horse with weak legs having a sea bath. These are but some of a colourful survey of the sport.

Casting a wider net the *Sporting Personalities* set issued by Gallaher covers the waterfront with a galaxy of stars. There is a typical portrait of the Hon. Dorothy Paget; the Marquis of Douglas and Clydesdale, the 'Boxing Marquis', son of the thirteenth Duke of Hamilton, who among many feats was the chief pilot of the Mount Everest Air Expedition of 1933 and the first to fly over the peak; Sir Malcolm Campbell and Kid Berg; Tom Walls of 'April the Fifth' fame and Cliff Bastin, Arsenal's international outside-left; Frank Furlong, the amateur rider who won the Grand National on Reynoldstown and Dixie Dean of Everton; C.W.A. Scott, who set up record flights from England to Australia and Jim Sullivan, the Wigan Rugby League giant; Tom Webster, the cartoonist; Harold Abrahams, athlete and later wireless sports commentator; Sir Harry Preston; Melbourne Inman; George Allison who succeeded Herbert Chapman as Arsenal manager: Ivor Anthony, jockey and trainer; E.H. Temme, the first man to swim the English Channel both ways; Freddie Dixon and Percy Fender; Sir Walter Gilbey and Patsy Hendren; Ted "Bossy" Phelps and Alex James; Frank Woolley and Lord Burghley; Frank Chester, who officiated in more Test matches than any other umpire; Captain George Eyston and Len Harvey; Fred Darling and Jack Hobbs; Herbert Chapman and Lord Lonsdale. These are but a selection from this remarkable gallery of sportsmen.

Somewhat surprisingly golf was neglected. Wills in 1924 issued a set of large cards on golf courses with excellent views of the principal courses and clubhouses. In 1927 Churchmans produced a series of *Famous Golfers* with remarkably clear photographic studies of past champions like John Ball and George Duncan. Four years later the same firm issued caricatures by Mel of *Prominent Golfers* like Archie Compston Abe Mitchell, Walter Hagen, James Braid, Bobby Jones, Leo Diegel and Henry Cotton. More practical hints came from Players in 1939 with an instructional set of 25 showing how shots were played by such professionals as Alfred Padgham, Reginald and Charles Whitcombe, Dai Rees, Arthur Lacey, George Duncan, Bill Davies, Richard Burton and Percy Alliss.

Boxing and wrestling were popular. Ogdens issued *Pugilists and Wrestlers* in 1909–10. *Wrestling and Ju-Jitsu* by Players followed in 1911, a do-it-yourself series in self-defence. Churchman's *Boxing* in 1922 was interesting, but the best were the *Boxing Personalities* in 1938 that featured 50 of the world's outstanding fistic figures, men like Georges Carpentier, Gene Tunney, Henry Armstrong, Tommy Farr, Joe Louis, Larry Gains and Jack Dempsey. Snooker and billiards were minority interests. Robert Sinclair of Newcastle featured Willie Smith in 1928. Ogdens had *Billiards* by Tom Newman in the same year, followed six years later with *Trick Billiards*. Lambert and Butler catered for winter sports enthusiasts with an issue in 1914 featuring curling, ski-ing, sledging and ice-skating. The North and Midlands interests were considered by Ogdens in 1931 with a series of *Racing Pigeons* featuring the champion birds including San Sebastian, winner of the race from the Faroe Islands to Peterborough, later bought by J.B. Joel for a record price.

A different type of subject-matter was covered by Churchmans' *Sporting Trophies* which shows the cups, vases and trophies awarded to the winners of the main sporting events, including the FA Cup, Wimbledon trophies, the Diamond Sculls, Rugby League Championship Cup, the Americas Cup, Grand Challenge Cup and the Waterloo Cup. In 1934 Churchmans produced an issue in colour of *Racing Greyhounds* with the sub-title 'Registered with the National Greyhound Racing Club'. It shows 50 outstanding greyhounds including Mick the Miller, Seldom Led, and Wild Woolley. An issue of general interest came from Gallagher with a series of *Champions*. It lived up to its name with such varied figures as the Hon. Michael Scott, the oldest golfer (at fifty-five) to win the British Amateur Championship; Jim Mollison, pioneer airman;

Eric Phelps, son of "Bossy"; Earl Howe, veteran Brooklands driver; Joe Davis and Harold Larwood; Dorothy Round and G.H. Stainforth, who held the early world air speed record. Stephen Mitchell produced *Old Sporting Prints* which graphically records a mixed bag of sporting occasions, winners of classic races and a glimpse of 'A Match at Hambledon played on Broadhalfpenny Down' in 1777. A unique set was produced by Players of *Straight Line Caricatures*. The artist was Alick Ritchie. Limiting himself to straight lines, he created uncanny likenesses of a wide range of public figures. In the sporting category appear Lord Hawke, Sir Hugo Cunliffe-Owen, Jack Hobbs, Steve Donoghue, Earl of Derby, Aga Khan and the Earl of Lonsdale with Sir Thomas Lipton.

Four major sports are left. Of these lawn tennis was neglected. Copes issued *Lawn Tennis Strokes* in 1924 with Players adding a similar set in 1936 entitled *Tennis*. Outstanding players of that time are shown playing specific strokes with instructional tips. The figures in white stand out against a green background. The strokes have been frozen by the camera so the action is genuine. Fred Perry and Mrs Fearnley-Whittingstall demonstrate the service; Senorita Lizana the running forehand drive; Miss Kay Stammers the forehand drive; Bunny Austin a typical backhand drive, likewise Jack Crawford, the Australian Davis Cup player; Miss Dorothy Round plays an effortless low backhand drive; Baron von Cramm, the backhand drive; Miss Helen Jacobs a low backhand volley; Adrian Quist an overhead volley; Harry Hopman, a backhand lob-volley; Donald Budge the half-volley; Miss Betty Nuthall a standing smash; and the inimitable Jean Borotra, known as the 'Bounding Basque', playing his favourite lob-volley.

Rugby football is represented by three splendid issues. In 1935 Churchmans produced *Rugby Internationals* showing 50 outstanding players like Peter Cranmer, Wilfred Wooller, Cliff Jones, R.C.S. Dick, D.A. Kendrew and Idwal Rees. Perhaps more interesting are two sets by Players of *Football Caricatures* – one by 'Mac', the other by 'Rip'. The range is shared by soccer and rugby. The latter is represented by such players as I.S. Smith, the Scottish wing three-quarter; J.B. Ganly, Irish international; K.A. Sellar, England full-back; J.S. Tucker, England forward; B.R. Turnbull, Welsh centre three-quarter; H. Waddell of Scotland; R. Cove-Smith and W.W. Wakefield, both England captains and internationals of rare distinction; M. Sugden and G.V. Stephenson of Ireland. In many ways these caricatures, not unkind in treatment, make a greater impact than straight portraits. Another unusual set issued by Hills' is the *All Blacks* of 1930, a rare collector's item.

Soccer personalities have been popular since the earliest sets. Copes of Liverpool began the vogue with some 500 cards titled *Noted Footballers*. In 1907 Cohen of London released a set of 60 *Football Club Captains* followed by *Heroes of Sport* in which well-known soccer players rubbed shoulders with Ranji and W.G. Grace. Murrays of Belfast produced *Footballers*, a set of 100 cards that recalled such stars as Steve Bloomer of Derby County and Billy Gillespie. The 1899 Kinnear's issue of 23 *Footballers and Club Colours* is rare. Ogdens had *Football Club Colours* in 1906, whilst about the same time Percy Cadle of Cardiff released their 20 *Footballers*.

Gallahers went one better in 1910 with 100 *Association Football Club Colours* followed later with a monochrome set of 100 *Famous Footballers* that featured such old-timers as Elisha Scott, the Irish goalkeeper and colourful Liverpool player, Sam Wadsworth, Frank Womack and Charlie Buchan. The year 1926 saw the release of 50 *Famous Footballers* in colour by the same manufacturer and once more we saw such giants as Alex Jackson, Clem Stephenson, Hugh Gallacher, Joe Smith and Bob Kelly. Two years later, 1928, marked a set that has historical interest. *Footballers in Action* were scenes taken from League matches. Hills had a fine set in 1923 of 50 *Famous Footballers* featuring men like Andy Ducat and Pat Hendren, already famous as cricketers. Three years later Players produced *Football Caricatures* that were shared with rugby. Two long-forgotten Merseyside professionals, Harry Chambers and Sam Chedzoy, are again remembered. Players' *Footballers 1928* were in water-colour, again shared with rugby. Two men of note were David Jack and Harry Healless of Blackburn Rovers, whilst rugby had Windsor Lewis of Wales and G.P.S. Macpherson of Scotland. In 1930 the same firm produced a set, now rare, of *Football Association Cup Winners*, a visual record of each winning team between 1893 and 1929. Four years later Players produced an instructional series, *Hints on Association Football*. That same year Stephen Mitchell became parochial with an issue on *Scottish Footballers* headlining Jack Harkness, Jimmy M'Grory and George Stevenson. In 1935 Wills came up with *Association Footballers* which had names like Sam Weaver, Raich Carter and Eric Brook.

The same year saw the Carreras coloured set of *Famous Footballers* with players like Warney Cresswell of Everton, Ernest Blenkinsop of

Liverpool, Eddie Hapgood, Dixie Dean, Cliff Bastin and Alex James justifying the title. Ardath matched the issue with 50 *Famous Footballers* that included Harry Hibbs, Willis Edwards and Eddie Hapgood. More *Famous Footballers* appeared in 1936 from Godfrey Phillips. Their stars had Ted Sagar and Alf Young. Three years later, Wills released their last issue, *Association Footballers*. Churchmans had a set with the same title showing Tommy Lawton of Everton, Willie Hall of Spurs, Don Welsh of Charlton Athletic and Stan Cullis of Wolves. Churchmans produced a Second Series later that year in which youthful Sam Bartram and Bill Shankly are pictured. The war cut short the flood of issues, apart from Dicksons Orde of Farnham who released a set of 50 *Footballers* in 1960 featuring players like Brian Clough, George Eastham, Nat Lofthouse, Tom Finney and Bob Stokoe. Three years later Barratts added another 50 *Famous Footballers* that included Billy Wright, Denis Law and Gordon Banks. In their entirety these soccer cards constitute a remarkable cavalcade of the players and an accurate commentary on the history of the game.

Cricket offers a rich selection of issues, some of the earlier ones having a rarity value of several hundred pounds. The 1896 Wills set recalls Lord Hawke, F.S. Jackson and W.G. Grace. The same manufacturers in 1901 produced a *Cricket* series followed by *Cricketers*, reproducing some of England's outstanding players of that decade. Two sets came from Scotland in 1912. F. and J. Smith issued a set of 50 cricketers and another featuring the Australian tourists. Ireland was next on the scene, Murrays of Belfast producing a mixture of *Cricketers and Footballers*. There was no shortage of choice at that time. Godfrey Phillips' set of 200 *Cricketers* was excellent. Taddy and Company also offered 200 *County Cricketers*, along with Ogdens' *Cricketers and Sportsmen* and Hills' well-known *Famous Cricketers* series in monochrome.

In 1923 Hills excelled themselves with the choice set of 40 *Famous Cricketers*. The names speak for themselves: Wilfred Rhodes, George Gunn, Phil Mead, Percy Fender, Cecil Parkin, A.P.F. Chapman, Herbert Sutcliffe, A.E.R. Gilligan, Archie McLaren and the Hon. Lionel Tennyson. This was matched the following year when 50 more *Famous Cricketers* were added, including the South African touring side and the likes of Gubby Allen and Maurice Leyland. Ogdens retaliated with *Cricket 1926* which pictured the Australian tourists plus A.W. Carr, Percy Holmes, Jack Gregory, Patsy Hendren, E.A. McDonald, Grimmett,

Instructive studies of famous bowlers in action that interest every cricket purist.

Mailey, Macartney, Ponsford, Oldfield and Woodfull, names that remind us how rich that period was in cricketing talent. In 1928 Wills featured action studies in *Cricketers* with a Second Series the following year. Churchmans introduced a change with *Famous Cricket Colours*, an issue of 25 that reproduced every First Class County, Oxford and Cambridge 'blues', England and the MCC, along with the caps and badges of the touring sides of England, South Africa and Australia. Also collectable are Players' *Cricketers* caricatured by Rip with faithful likenesses. From

The 1926 issue of Cricketers from Players were caricatures by *Rip* that caught quite remarkable likenesses with characteristic mannerisms.

1926 until 1936 Players released sets that included the Australians. The 1934 issue in pastels was one of the best and featured men like Walter Hammond and R.E.S. Wyatt. The last set by this manufacturer on cricketers was in 1938, a year when Ogdens released a good black and white set *Prominent Cricketers of 1938* in which are seen R.W.V. Robins, Harold Gimlett, A.B. Sellers and Alf Gover. Then in 1956 Kane Products issued cards recalling the leading players of that year. Of all these sets my preference would go to Gallaher's series of 100 *Famous Cricketers* featuring photographic action studies of men like W.G. Quaife, John Gunn, B.J.T. Bosanquet, V.W.C. Jupp, J.C. White, G.G. Macaulay, Richard Tyldesley, Ranji, F. Watson, Duleepsinhji, C.B. Fry, Maurice Tate, J.W. Hearn, J.W.H.T. Douglas, Pelham Warner, Jack Hobbs, George Gunn, H.L. Collins, J.S. Ryder ... the full line-out is virtually a visual Who's Who of the golden age of cricket.

Finally, for those who tire of strenuous activities, Copes produced a set on how to play the *Game of Poker*.

CHAPTER 18

THE APPEAL OF THE SEARCH

The foregoing chapters have shown how prolific is the field for speci-alised collectors of sporting items. The scope is wide, the price range remarkably flexible with something for every purse. Many of the sub-jects are simple and naive in treatment and often requiring background knowledge to appreciate their significance. It is pieces such as these that sometimes trigger-off moods of nostalgia known only by hearsay. The fascination of collecting memorabilia of another era has its own distinc-tive appeal. The gold of the past was perhaps never more than gilt, but life then seemed full of glitter for the quality and pace of living was so different. It was an age made attractive by leisurely tempo and elegance of style that was copied by foreigners. Spectators in paintings and prints of Ascot, Goodwood and Newmarket and even in earlier scenes at illegal bare-fisted fights, were shown in top-hats with curving brims, narrow bands flat-edged over the eyes and worn at a rakish angle; waisted short coats with low openings in front; shirt-fronts wide with collars loose and slightly starched; heavy-knit ties with dangling ends; trousers pale strawberry roan with ends turned down; boots fashionably pointed. Add further touches of tweed caps and spats, long moustaches with ends trailing almost to the shoulders, and hair curling and frizzled with hot tongs and stiffened with bear grease. The golden coins are melted down, the spirit-lamps are out, Victorias and barouches are no more, yet that atmosphere, demoded as frangipani, still clings to many sport-ing items.

As a postscript I have selected ten further items, most of which were found in country antique shops, available to any collector and not expensive, with appeal to the realist as well as the dilettante, irrational but irresistible temptations that nag true collectors.

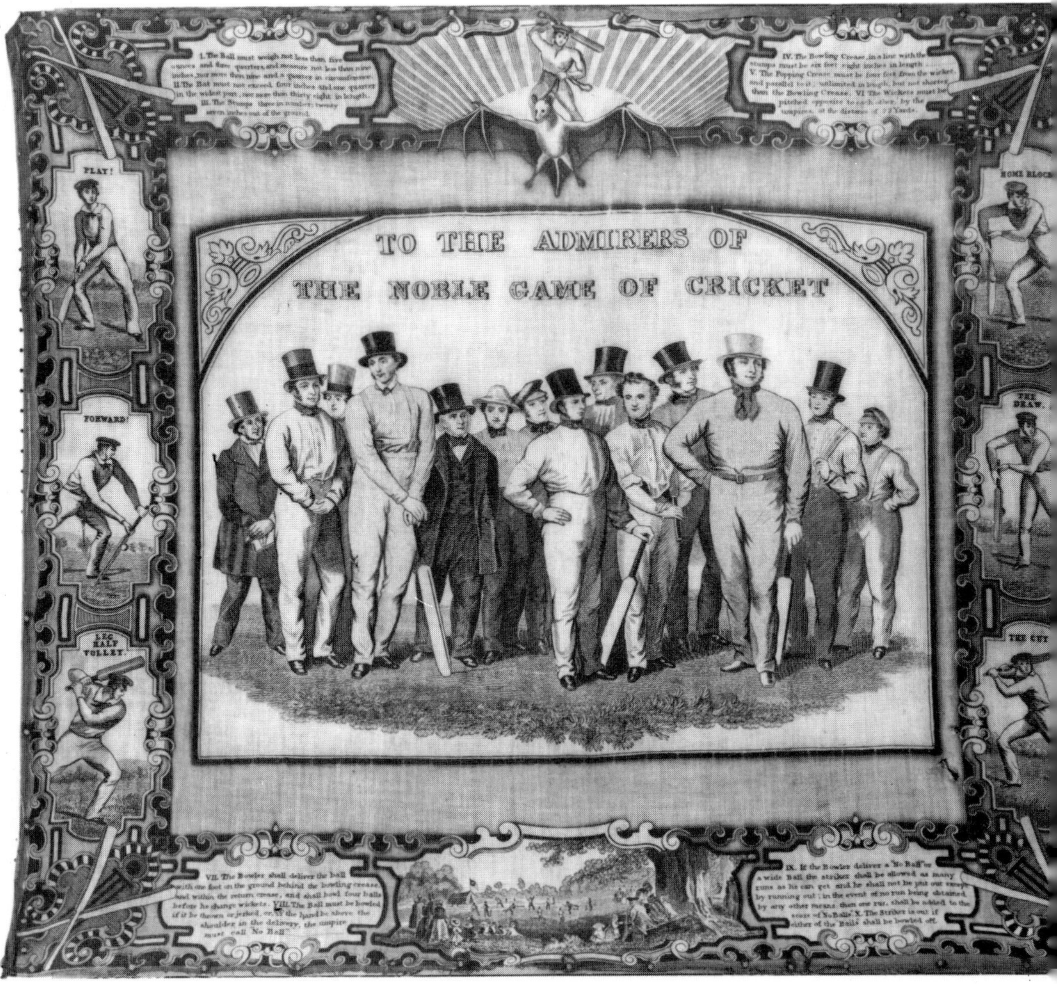

Interesting compilation of early cricket rules, tactical tips and group of old-time cricketing personalities.

1. Set of nineteenth-century cricketing belt clasps decorated with batting, bowling and wicket-keeping figures.

2. Large clay pipe with raised motifs on the bowl showing a soccer and rugby match in progress, supported by out-stretched football boot with the ball at the toe – c. 1890.

3. Plaque of Lord Hawke, doyen of Yorkshire cricket for forty

160

years, outstanding administrator, autocrat and captain of England.

4. Plated figure modelled on G.O. Smith, the Victorian centre-forward, who captained England and played in the classic Corinthian side of 1900.

5. Bilston and Battersea enamel box with golfing scene on the hinged lid showing the first green of the Old Course at St

Typical Walton group showing sportsman, pointer with obliging birds.

Early twentieth-century cricketing game with W.G. Grace the dominant figure.

Andrews with the clubhouse of the Royal and Ancient and the Martyr's Monument in the background.

6. Water-colour vignette portraits of F.R. Spofforth, the *Demon*, one of the fastest and most hostile of bowlers; J. McBlackham, the first great modern wicket-keeper; M.A. Noble, Australian all-rounder who captained Australia in 15 of his 42 Tests; Victor Trumper, Sidney Barnes and Tom Richardson; three cricket legends – Don Bradman, Jack Hobbs and Wilfred Rhodes; and W.G. Grace, the GOM of English cricket.

7. Boat Race mug marking the 150th anniversary of the Ox-

ford and Cambridge duel with a view of the first encounter and Arms of both universities.

8. Commemorative football mug titled *International Heroes* featuring W.J. Bassett (rugby) and Dan Doyle (soccer) with reverse side showing a soccer match in progress with several players enjoying fisticuffs on the quiet.

9. Watercolour drawn by Arnold Denman on a plate by H. Bunbury dated 1823 showing billiard players around a table with the garb, mannerisms and features of a Rowlandson-type caricature.

10. Glass decanter commissioned by the Marylebone Cricket Club in a limited edition of 100; engraved on the front in detailed outline is the Lord's pavilion.

Specialised collecting calls for patience and research to find out as much as possible about each piece, always remembering that acquiring in itself is not the main attraction. The real appeal is the search.

INDEX